Boxes & Chests

Boxes & Chests

How to Make and Decorate 15 Traditional Country Projects

Alan and Gill Bridgewater

STACKPOLE
BOOKS

Published by
STACKPOLE BOOKS
5067 Ritter Road
Mechanicsburg, PA 17055

Printed in the United States of America

10 9 8 7 6 5 4 3

FIRST EDITION

Cover design by Tina Marie Hill and Caroline M. Stover

Cover and color-section photographs by Mike Lewis Photography

Black-and-white photographs and line drawings by the authors

Library of Congress Cataloging-in-Publication Data

Bridgewater, Alan.
    Boxes and chests : how to make and decorate 15
traditional country projects / Alan and Gill
Bridgewater. — 1st ed.
        p.   cm.
    Includes bibliographical references.
    ISBN 0-8117-2559-6
    1. Woodwork.   2. Painted wooden boxes.
3. Decoration and ornament, Rustic.   I. Bridgewater,
Gill.   II. Title.
TT200.B75   1997
684´.08—dc20   96–27435
                            CIP

To Peter Bridgewater

For his help over the years

Contents

Acknowledgments

We would like to thank all the manufacturers who have provided us with tools and supplies: Tim Effrem, President, Wood Carvers Supply (woodcarving tools); Jim Brewer, Research and Marketing Manager, Freud (Forstner drill bits); William Nelsen, President, Foredom Electric (power tools); John P. Jodkin, Vice President, Delta International Machinery (band saws); Dawn Fretz, Marketing Assistant, De-Sta-Co. (clamps); Paragon Communications, Evo-Stick (PVA adhesive); Frank Cootz, Public Relations, Ryobi America Corp (thickness planer); and Glen Tizzard, Draper Tools UK.

We would also like to thank all of the anonymous woodworkers of the past—furniture makers, homesteaders, home builders, village carpenters, and the like—who spent time making boxes, chests, trunks, trays, and coffers in wood. We all recognize and admire those wonderfully painted Pennsylvania German chests, ornately carved Massachusetts chests, and distinctively designed boxes and chests of the Shakers, Mennonites, and Mormons. We are familiar with their overall design and form, and we more or less, know when, where, and why they were made. But, the sad truth is that we know little or nothing about the individuals who made them. So the next time you get to see a beautiful chest in a museum or a small personalized chip-carved box at a flea market, ask yourself these questions. Was it made by a young man for his girl? Was it made by a young apprentice starting out in life? Was that salt box decorated by the woman of the house? What was the significance of the date or initials to the person who carved them on the piece? Study the joints, admire the design, run your finger tips over the wood, and then give the maker due credit.

Introduction

Wooden boxes and chests are traditionally all about us. We are placed in boxlike cradles and cribs when we are born, we are buried in coffins when we die, and during all the years in between just about everything we eat, drink, wear, or otherwise value spends a good part of its life being protected, hoarded, hidden, or exhibited in some sort of box or chest.

Characteristically, a box or chest must have a fixed structure or frame with at least one movable panel. The simplest box is made up of six sides, one of which is a lid. The lid may slide, pivot, or be fastened with metal hinges, pins, hasps, latches, or catches. A chest is best defined as being no more and no less than the big brother to the box.

Wooden boxes and chests are at the very root of the European and American furniture-making tradition. In the twelfth century, massive cut-from-a-tree chests were set up in churches for collecting money. Later, in the fourteenth century, chests were made from slabs and so became more portable. In the fifteenth century, they were paneled up to include one or more drawers. In the sixteenth and seventeenth centuries, they became more ornate and were used for special ceremonial purposes. Thus box and chest forms gradually evolved to become chests with drawers, chests of drawers, sideboards, bureaus, and all the other pieces of cabinet furniture we know today.

In America, boxes and chests were often the only physical link with the mother country. Whereas the emigrants necessarily had to sell most of their possessions when they left Europe, a good number of their boxes and chests traveled with them. And naturally enough, when these new Americans eventually set up home, so the European boxes and chests became treasured heirlooms that were passed down through the family. In the early American context, the box or chest is more than just a piece of furniture—it symbolizes the great American struggle for home and hearth, and it signifies stability and permanence. No sooner did the settlers put down roots than they immediately started to build boxes. One could argue that they had no choice but to make all manner of functional containers—and that of course is true—but if the task was simply a mundane chore, why did they make such a joyous array of forms? Fancy little carved and pierced wall boxes were fashioned for candles and cutlery, huge sumptuous chests made for storing clothes, large dowry chests built and painted to mark special events, and so on. They spent long hours creating all manner of beautifully made and vigorously decorated box and chest forms. Such boxes and chests are more than just functional containers—they are folk and family pleasures, needs, and histories set down in wood.

From the woodworker's viewpoint, there is something magical about traditional box and chest making; it's almost as if the ability to make these archetypal forms is the measure of the woodworker's skill. Chest and box making is likely the best introduction into the craft of woodworking that you will ever find, and if you can make a well-fitted box or chest, then the rest is easy!

The various projects in *Boxes & Chests* can be made by woodworkers at all levels, from the raw beginner with a minimal tool kit to the more accomplished woodworker who wants to make something extra special. You don't have to be a woodworking guru—you just have to be enthusiastic.

We set the various boxes and chests in context and show you in detail how to make fifteen different traditional forms, from a simple candle box to a magnificent painted chest, and a wide range of exciting, challenging, and intriguing box and chest projects in between. Each project opens with a small introduction describing the background of the piece, and then we tell you all you need to know to make the project, with step-by-step text, photographs, and hands-on-tool pen illustrations, along with gridded working drawings. If you want to know how to use a particular tool or make a certain joint, the Woodshop Techniques section will show you how. If you want to create your own designs based on historical boxes and chests, the Inspiration Gallery will help you on your way.

So there you go. We wish you all the best in your venture!

New England Knife Tray

A shallow tray traditionally used for holding cutlery.
Shaped with a scroll saw, plane, and knife; jointed with saw and chisel;
glued and nailed; painted and waxed.

Rich or poor, just about every early American household had a container for holding their knives, forks, and spoons. A wealthy family might well have had a couple of boxes, say a splendid affair for the special silver—perhaps a box made of mahogany inlaid with exotic woods—and a more ordinary box for the everyday cutlery. Poor folks would like as not make do with a shallow, square-sided box knocked up from scraps of crate wood.

The knife box in the project would have been owned by a more prosperous family. Although the original is only made from pine, the splayed sides and the fancy fretted center board with the integral handle hole suggest that it was made by a professional woodworker. All in all, it is a delightful box—plain, simple, and altogether beautiful!

Design, structure, and technique

The knife tray measures about 16 inches long across the span of the handle, 12 inches across the width of the end, and 7³/4 inches high. The total base measures about 14¹/2 inches long and 11³/4 inches wide (see 1-1). The center board is jointed into the end boards by means of a housing slot or channel, and the base and the long, low side slats are fixed with roundheaded brass pins. The whole thing is nailed together, given a thin green wash, swiftly rubbed down to remove the sharp corners and grain hairs, and then waxed.

Wood and Materials

This knife box is unpretentious and homely, and the grain will show through the green wash, so it is best to go for an easy-to-find, attractive, strong-grained wood like pine.

For this project you need the following:

- A prepared ¹/2-inch-thick board at 8 inches wide and 17 inches long for the central handle spine.
- Two ³/8- to ¹/2-inch-thick boards at 6 inches wide and 12¹/2 inches long for the ends.
- Two ¹/4-inch-thick boards at about 3 inches wide and 16 inches long for the two side slats.
- A selection of ³/8- to ¹/2-inch-thick boards at about 15 inches long to make up the 11¹/2-inch width of the base.
- Some ³/4-inch-long round-headed brass nails.
- Leaf green watercolor paint.
- Beeswax furniture polish.
- PVA glue.

Fig. 1-1. Working drawing, top, *at a grid scale of 1 square to 1 inch and* bottom, *4 squares to 1 inch. Note the housing channel joint for the center board, and the simple butt joints for the corners and for the base.*

Fig. 1-2. Cutting guide, at a grid scale of 1 square to 1 inch. Note that all pieces should be cut oversized and then reduced to a good fit.

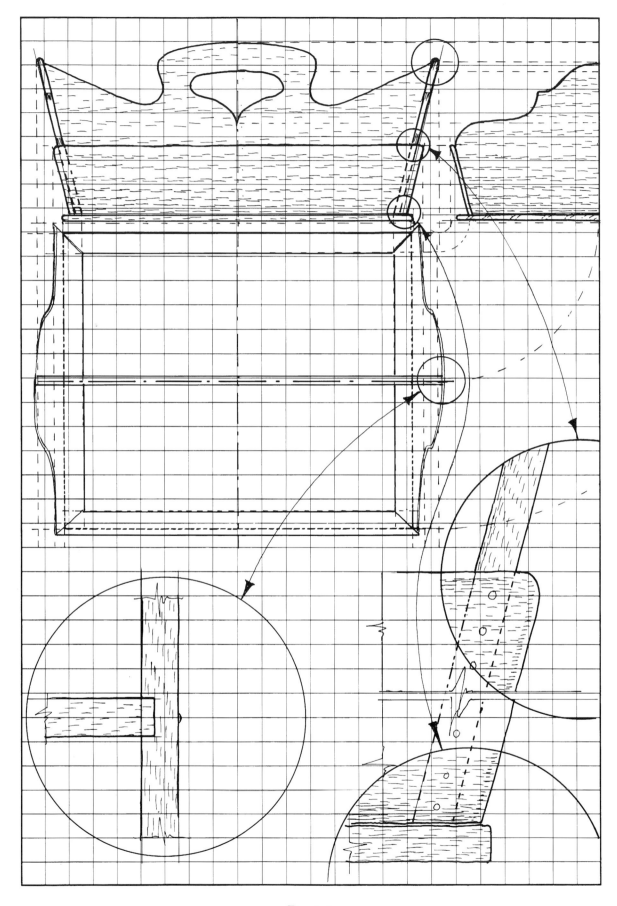

Fig. 1-1

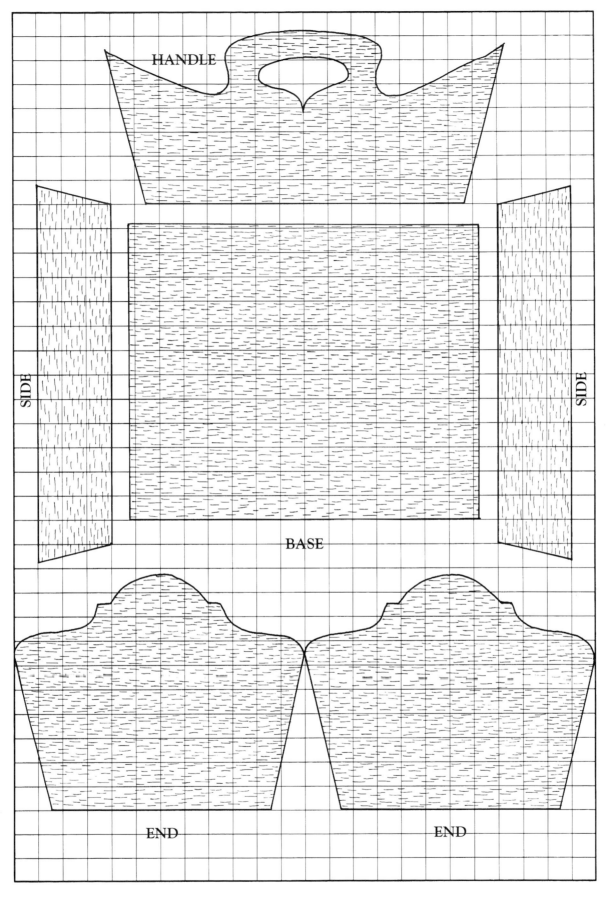

HANDLE

SIDE

SIDE

BASE

END

END

Fig. 1-2

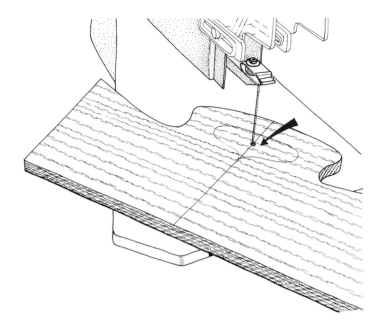

Fig. 1-3. *Make sure that the blade is well tensioned with the teeth pointing down toward the workpiece. A correctly tensioned blade should ping when strummed.*

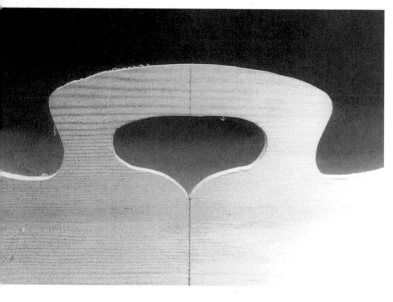

Fig. 1-4. *It's important that the area around the handle hole be free from splits. To prevent this, you can use a thicker piece of wood—say about 3/4 inch—or laminate two thin sheets so that the grain is crossed.*

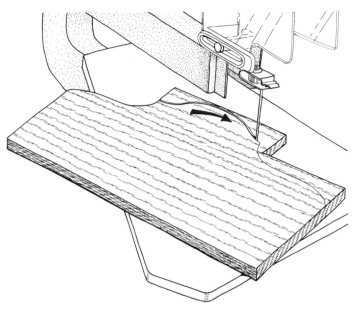

Fig. 1-5. *Work at an easy pace, all the while being ready to feed the blade with the line of next cut. Be mindful that if your piece of wood has a grain made up of alternate hard and soft areas, the blade is likely to "run away" through the soft areas.*

SUGGESTED TOOLS AND SUPPLIES

- A small band saw.
- An electric scroll saw, fretsaw, or coping saw.
- A small gents saw.
- A pencil, ruler, and pair of dividers.
- An adjustable angle square.
- A good sharp knife for cleaning up the curves (we use a Swedish sloyd knife).
- A 1/2-inch-wide bevel-edged chisel.
- A hand drill with a 1/4-inch bit.
- A small block plane.
- A sheet of graph paper.
- A sheet of tracing paper.
- A watercolor brush.
- All the usual workshop tools and materials, such as 80-120 grit sandpaper and scissors.

CONSTRUCTION

Layout and Fretting

1. First, familiarize yourself with the project. Take a good long look at the project photographs (see color section) and working drawings (see 1-1 and 1-2), spend time study-

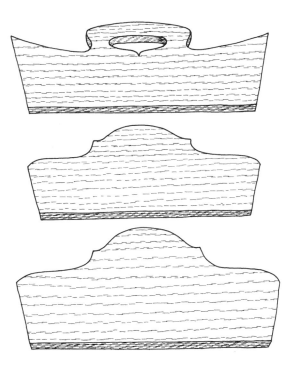

Fig. 1-6. Set the three component parts out on the bench and check them over to make sure that they are free from splits and twists.

Fig. 1-7. If you butt the workpiece up against a piece of waste, you will be able to run the saw cut straight through without damaging the edge of the wood.

Fig. 1-8. Use a bevel-edged chisel to skim the bottom of the channel down to a flat finish. Take two cuts at an angle, and then skim the resultant peak down to a smooth finish.

ing the way the box has been worked and put together. If you can, visit a folk art museum and look at similar boxes that were made between 1800 and 1920.

2.   When you have a clear understanding of the project and have selected your wood, draw the shape of the center board and one end board at full size on paper and make a clear pencil tracing.

3.   Press-transfer the image onto the appropriate lengths of wood, and put in as many guidelines as you think necessary.

4.   Take a central spine board and drill a 1/4-inch hole through the enclosed handle area.

5.   Now move to the scroll saw and set to work fretting out the profile. When you come to the handle, unhitch the scroll saw blade, pass one end through the drilled hole, rehitch the blade, and then continue fretting (see 1-3). If you are a beginner, it's all simple enough, as long as the blade is well tensioned and you keep the wood moving.

6.   When you have sawn out the central board with its beautiful handle shape (see 1-4), refit the blade and move on to cutting the end boards (see 1-5).

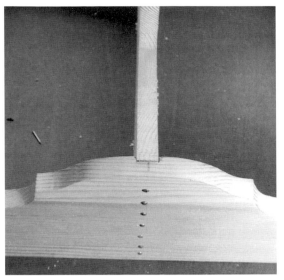

Fig. 1-9. Aim for a tight push-fit, with the top edge of the center board protruding out.

Fig. 1-10. Nail the end boards to the center board, and use a square to check that all of the boards are correctly aligned.

Cutting the Housing Slot

1. Having cut out the three boards that need to be fretted (see 1-6), take the two end boards and use pencil, ruler, and square to lay out the housing channel. The easiest procedure is to first establish the centerline with the square, and then set the thickness of the center board on the line. For example, if your center board is 1/2 inch thick, mark a 1/4-inch step-off to each side of the centerline at the top and bottom, extend the lines across the edge, and mark the depth of the housing.

2. Now mark out the channel with the knife. Then take the gents saw and very carefully set the channel in with two parallel cuts to the waste side of the guidelines. Sink them in to a depth of about 1/8 inch (see 1-7). Repeat this procedure for both end boards. It's helpful to clamp a piece of waste wood to use as a guide at the shoulder line. If the guide is the right height, the rib on the back of the saw will hit the guide and act as a stop.

3. Use the chisel to pare out the waste. Remove the bulk with a couple of straight through cuts angled toward the shoulder lines (see 1-8), and then hold the chisel flat down

and skim the bottom of the housing down to a clean finish.

Assembly and Finishing

1. Now test-fit the pieces (see 1-9) and see how the joints come together. If you have done a good job, the center board will be a nice tight push-fit.

2. Smear a small amount of glue on mating surfaces, then slide the center board in place and fit. Secure with the brass nails every 3/4 inch or so along the centerline (see 1-10). If you are worried about the wood splitting, you can drill pilot holes for the nails.

3. Use the block plane to chamfer the splayed side edges of the end boards so that they butt cleanly onto the slats. This is a slightly tricky procedure, as you have to get all four corners just right, so go at it nice and easy, all the while stopping to check the squareness of the total structure.

4. When you have a fair fit, smear a small amount of glue on mating faces and secure the slats directly to the chamfered edges with nails at about 3/4-inch intervals (see 1-11). Again, you can drill pilot holes before nailing to prevent splitting.

Fig. 1-11. Have the ends set back slightly so that the slats lap over by about 3/4 inch.

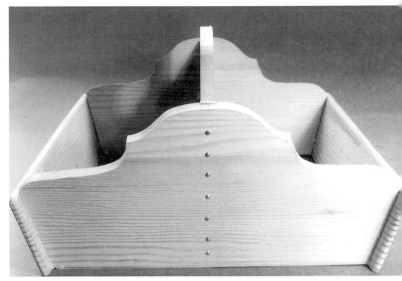

Fig. 1-12. When you have achieved the basic structure, use a block plane and sandpaper to work the bottom edges until they accurately meet the base.

5. If all is well, the slat ends should lap over the end pieces by about 1/2 to 3/4 inch (see 1-12).

6. When you have completed a stable structure (see 1-13), glue and nail the base slats in place and sand all the edges to a rounded finish.

7. Clean up the debris, move to a dustfree area, and give the whole works a thin wash of green watercolor. Allow to dry, then sand the entire piece smooth, and wax to a dull sheen finish.

VARIATIONS

• If you want to simplify the project, you can set the long slat sides at right angles to the base. This eliminates the need to chamfer the end board edges.

• If you want to shortcut the housing channel procedure, you can use a little router plane rather than the chisel. The design of the hand router plane ensures that the cut is level every time.

• If you want an authentic folk paint effect, you can use milk paints rather than watercolors. We use a mix of kids' powder color and dried milk powder.

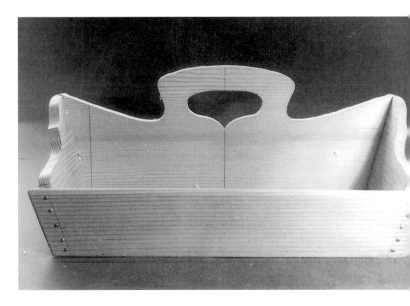

Fig. 1-13. Rub the top end of the housing joint down so that the junction between the center board and the end boards makes a curve that is pleasing to the eye.

Pennsylvania Book Box

A book-shaped box used traditionally for holding trinkets.
Cut on a band saw; shaped with a plane, knife, gouge, and scraper;
mitered on the band saw; glued and nailed; painted with acrylics and waxed.

Small decorative wooden containers were very popular in early Pennsylvania households. If the number of museum examples are anything to go by, every room in the house must have been aglow with all manner of brightly painted boxes. Our beautiful little box draws its inspiration from an original that was made in Pennsylvania in about 1835. Although we can't say for sure what this particular box was used for, we believe it was made as a special gift—perhaps from the bridegroom to the bride—to accompany the dowry chest. The book shape with its secret compartment suggests that it was designed to hold special treasures, like letters and small love tokens.

DESIGN, STRUCTURE, AND TECHNIQUE

This book-shaped box measures about 5$1/2$ inches high, 4$1/2$ inches from the back of the spine to the edge of the covers, and 2$1/4$ inches in total thickness (see 2-3).

The design of this box is somewhat unusual in that the glue-and-nails construction is simple, but the carving and decoration are relatively sophisticated. The museum original is simply nailed together without any attempt at jointing, and yet the carving and painting are to a very high standard.

The box lid is very cleverly designed. The cover is cut with mitered edges and worked in such a way that it can be slid into place to make a secret lid. All things considered, we get the feeling that the original box was one of a kind, perhaps made by someone who enjoyed the designing, painting, and giving more than the woodworking.

WOOD AND MATERIALS

Though you might think that the choice of wood isn't too important—after all, the finished box is painted inside and out and the grain is completely hidden from view—the success of the project hinges on your choice of wood. It is vital that you use a tight-grained, knotfree, splinter-resistant wood—a wood that can be nailed without splitting and painted without the fear of resin stain. A traditional wood like maple or tulip poplar would be best.

For this project, and many of the others as well, the wood sizes and thicknesses are flexible. So, for example, although we specify 3/8-inch-thick wood for the cover of this box, you might use, say, 1/2-inch-thick wood and modify all the sizes to suit. Note that all measurements given allow a small amount for cutting waste.

Fig. 2-1. Top, working drawing, at a grid scale of 2 squares to 1 inch. Front, side, and bottom views, plus a cross-section detail. Bottom, painting design, at 4 grid squares to 1 inch. Note the symmetry of the individual forms as well as the total design.

Fig. 2-2. Cutting guide, at a scale of 2 squares to 1 inch. Note that sizes and thicknesses can be modified.

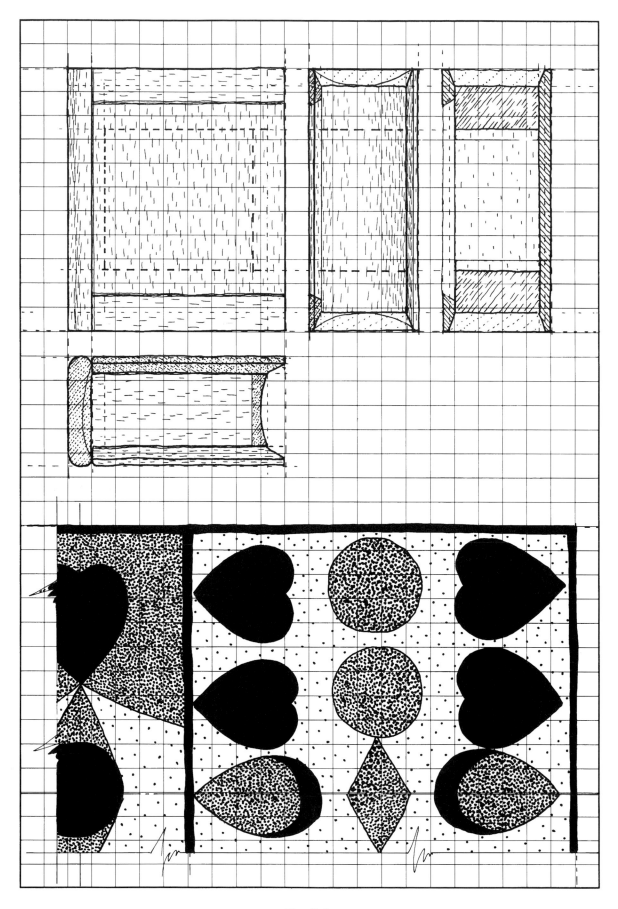

Fig. 2-1

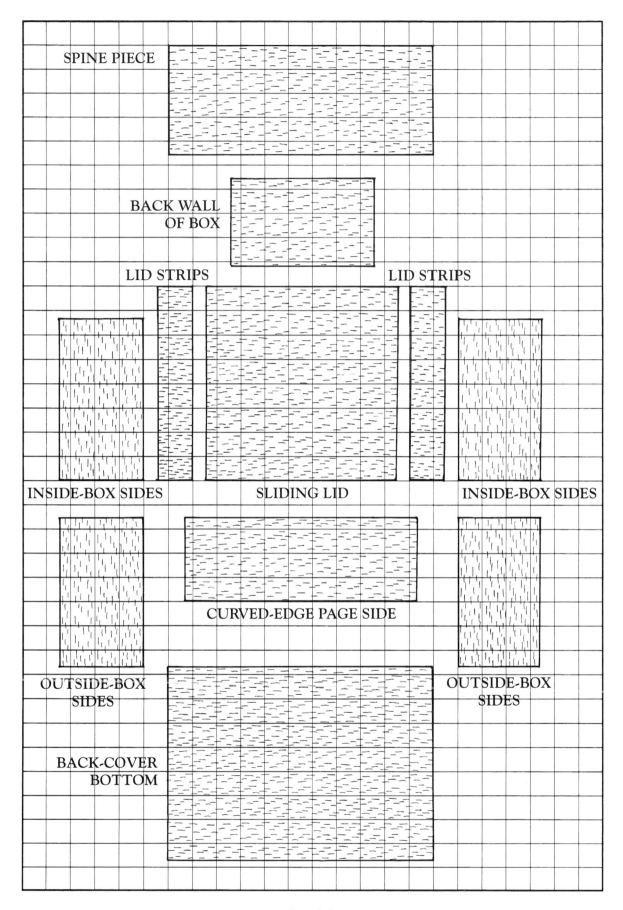

SPINE PIECE

BACK WALL
OF BOX

LID STRIPS   LID STRIPS

INSIDE-BOX SIDES   SLIDING LID   INSIDE-BOX SIDES

CURVED-EDGE PAGE SIDE

OUTSIDE-BOX
SIDES

OUTSIDE-BOX
SIDES

BACK-COVER
BOTTOM

Fig. 2-2

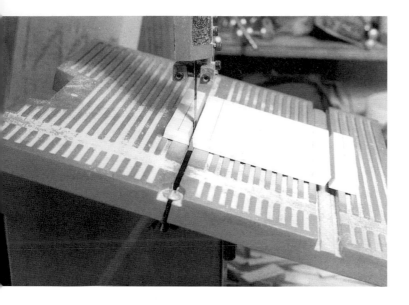

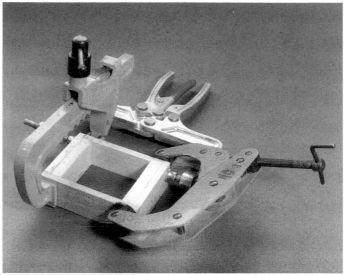

Fig. 2-3. When cutting the miter on the band saw, make sure that the inside box face is uppermost and the cuts are mirror-imaged to each other.

Fig. 2-5. Make sure that the surfaces are clean and free from grease, then smear glue on mating surfaces and clamp up. Tighten up until a thin bead of glue oozes from the joint line. Do not squeeze out too much glue, or you will create a weak joint.

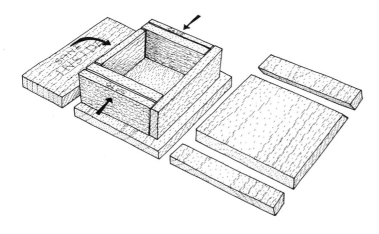

Fig. 2-4. Set the seven component parts out on the bench, check them over for squareness, and mark and number all the mating faces that need to be glued. Make sure that you don't get the miters the wrong way around.

For this project you need the following:
• Two 3/8-inch-thick boards at 6 inches long and 4 1/2 inches wide for the back and front cover boards.
• A 1/2-inch-thick piece at 6 inches long and 2 inches wide for the spine.
• A selection of scrap pieces between 1/4 and 1/2 inch thick for the box frame.
• Wood filler.
• Matte white emulsion paint.
• Acrylic paints: yellow-orange, red, and black.
• Beeswax furniture polish.
• PVA glue.

SUGGESTED TOOLS AND SUPPLIES
• A small bench band saw with an adjustable table.
• A pencil, ruler, and pair of dividers.
• An adjustable angle square.
• A good, sharp knife for shaping the curves (we use a Swedish sloyd knife).
• A shallow-sweep straight gouge.
• A small block plane.

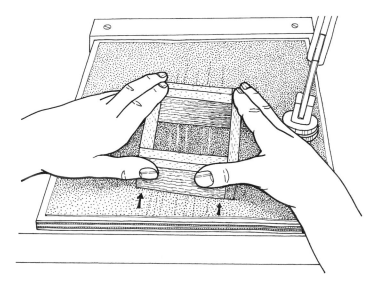

Fig. 2-6. Being careful not to round over the corners, run the faces of the frame down on the sanding board.

- A sheet of graph paper.
- A sheet of tracing paper.
- Watercolor brushes: broad and fine point.
- All the usual workshop tools and materials, such as sandpaper and scissors.

CONSTRUCTION

Layout and Preparation

1. First, familiarize yourself with the project. Take a good long look at the project photographs (see color section) and working drawings (see 2-1 and 2-2). Note how we have built the inside of the box—the frame—from a number of scrap pieces, with the top and bottom being made up from two thicknesses.

2. When you have selected your wood and maybe modified the design to suit your stock, lay out the shape of each part on the wood. Make sure that all the right angles are true.

3. Run the wood through the band saw, and then give the sawn parts a clean planed finish. Label all the parts with pencil so that you know how they relate to each other.

4. Take the front cover board and use the pencil, ruler, and square to mark the position of the two mitered cuts that go to make the sliding lid. They should be about 5/8 inch in from the cover edges on the inside box face, so that you are left with a lid about 4 inches wide as seen on the outside face.

Fig. 2-7. Set all the book cover parts around the frame and check for a good fit. The sliding lid needs to be held in place by the two overlapping miters.

Fig. 2-8. Use the block plane to carefully chamfer the inside edges of the cover. Butt the workpiece hard up against the bench stop to prevent the edges from splitting away.

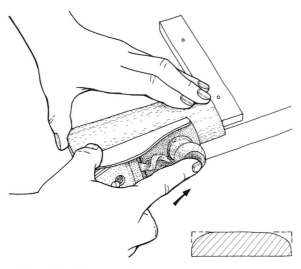

Fig. 2-9. Top, *now butt the spine piece hard up against the bench stop, and use the block plane to model the characteristic rounded shape. Bottom, cross-section diagram of the spine piece.*

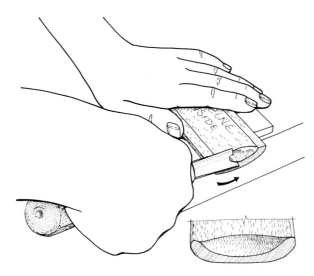

Fig. 2-10. Top, *butt the spine hard up against the bench stop with the inside face uppermost, and use the shallow-sweep straight gouge to hollow out the little concave shape. Remove the waste with a tight scooping cut. Bottom, a close-up detail showing how the inside ends of the spine need to be worked.*

Cutting the Miter and Building the Frame

1. Check that all your lines are true and well placed, then tilt the band saw worktable over so that it is at a good angle, set the front board down so that the inside box face is uppermost, and cut the two miters (see 2-3). This is pretty straightforward, as long as you make sure that the two cuts are mirror-imaged to each other.

2. Set the component parts out on the bench and make sure that they are well cut and clearly marked. You will have eleven parts in all: the back cover, the miter-edged lid, the two mitered strips, the spine, and the six pieces that go to make up the frame (see 2-4).

3. Use the plane and sandpaper to bring the six frame components to a good true finish, then test-fit the pieces. If all is correct, smear glue on mating faces and clamp up (see 2-5), checking with the square, and put to one side until the glue is set.

4. When the glue is dry, nail the frame together and rub all the faces of the frame down on a sanding board until they are smooth and true. Pay particular attention to the front and back faces—those faces of the frame that meet the inside book covers (see 2-6). To make a sanding board, use double-sided tape to fix a sheet of sandpaper to a piece of plywood. Secure the board to your bench with a bench holdfast.

Shaping with the Plane, Gouge, and Scraper

1. When you have finished the frame, test-fit all the pieces. Play around and see how the sliding lid and the two strips sit on the top of the frame so that the lid is held and contained by the two mitered edges (see 2-7).

2. Use the frame to draw in the position of the chamfered inside cover edges. If you have done it right, there will be a margin of about 3/8 inch wide around three edges. Run a pencil line around the cover edges to divide the thickness of the wood more or less in half. Use the frame to set out all the guidelines that go to make up the spine strip.

3. Nail one of the 3/8-inch-thick pieces of scrap to the bench to make a stop, butt the workpiece hard up against the stop, and use

the block plane to shave off the edge waste (see 2-8). When you are planing the end-grain edges, be careful that you don't split off the side grain at the end of the run.

4. Take the spine strip and plane the outside face to create the characteristic rounded spine shape that you see on old bound books. Aim for a nicely rounded shape where the spine rolls over at the edge, which is where the book cover hinges (see 2-9).

5. When you have shaped the outside of the spine strip, flip it over and use the gouge to hollow out the little curves that you see when the book is closed (see 2-10).

6. Set the frame in the bench vise so that the side opposite the spine is uppermost, and use the gouge to scoop out the characteristic concave hollow that you see on old bound books (see 2-11). Work across the grain, so as to avoid splitting the wood.

7. Use a convex profile metal scraper to bring the hollow to a good finish (see 2-12). Angle the scraper so that the curve fits the curved profile.

Assembly, Finishing, and Painting

1. Now test-fit all the pieces (see 2-13). If you are unhappy with the fit, now is the time to make adjustments.

2. Begin final assembly. First glue and nail the frame to the spine strip. Next, glue and nail the back cover to the frame. Then glue and nail the two mitered strips in place. Use the square to check for alignment, and then clamp up.

3. When the glue is set, cut the pretend miter lines on the back of the book to match the width of the sliding lid. Drive the nail heads below the surface, and cover with filler. Also wipe filler into all the joints.

4. Rub the whole project down so that it is smooth to the touch, then give all the surfaces a couple of thin coats of matte white paint and allow to dry. When dry, give all surfaces a couple of thin coats of yellow-orange paint.

5. When the paint is dry, use a pencil to press-transfer all the lines that go to make up the design from the tracing paper onto the wood (see 2-14). Don't be too painstaking—

Fig. 2-11. *Secure the frame in the vise, and use the gouge to carve the characteristic edge-of-pages shape. Work across the grain, with one hand holding and pushing, and the other hand controlling and braking.*

Fig. 2-12. *Hold the scraper at an angle to the run of the grain, and work with a stiff dragging stroke. Scrape in both directions.*

Fig. 2-13. Test-fit the pieces and plan the order of work. Pencil-mark all the mating faces.

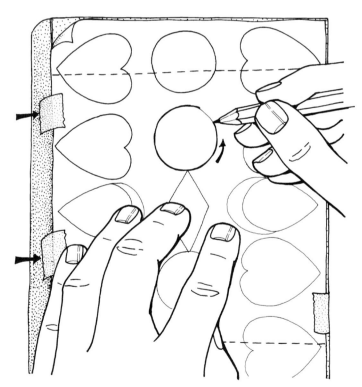

Fig. 2-14. Align the tracing paper on which you have traced the designs with the various guidelines on the wood, fix it in place with tabs of masking tape, and then press-transfer the traced design through to the wood with a pencil.

try to achieve swift immediate images. When you are happy that all is correct, block in the drawn shapes with the flat color, and use the black to line the edges of the cover.

6. Give the whole works a swift rubdown with the finest grade of sandpaper. Rub through the paint at wear areas to give the book a worn look. Then give all the surfaces a generous coat of beeswax polish, and burnish to a dull sheen finish.

TIPS

• Although cutting edge miters is easy enough, it's always a good idea to practice first with some scrap wood. Be warned: The band saw is potentially a very dangerous machine; don't try to cut the miters if you are tired or in a rush. In some instances, when you are working with very small pieces of wood, you will need to push the wood through with sticks rather than your fingers.

• The sliding lid needs to be an easy push-fit. If it is too tight, you could sand the mating faces of the mitered edge so that they are free from paint.

• We made a scraper by grinding the back edge of a metal paint comb down to a rounded profile (see 2-12). You could just as well reshape any piece of tempered steel.

• If you do the waxing when the acrylic paints have just dried, the paint will crawl slightly to give a very attractive and authentic aged and wrinkled effect.

VARIATIONS

• If you like the book idea but are not so keen about the size or the imagery, you could draw inspiration from a visit to a folk-art museum. If you make an appointment, you may be allowed to handle the exhibits so that you can study their construction.

• If you want to short-cut this project, you could make the pages from a solid block of wood, and drill the hollow with one or more large Forstner bits.

• If you want a more authentic finish, you would use traditional milk paints rather than acrylics.

• You could further the folk-art imagery by painting on the date and your initials.

New England Colonial Salt Box

A small box used traditionally for holding salt.
Cut on a scroll saw; shaped with a plane and knife; glued and nailed;
wire-brushed and waxed.

According to historical accounts, the settlers of old New England were masters of make-do and mend. Arriving in a wilderness, with a few woodcutting tools and nothing much else besides an almost unlimited supply of white pine, they rapidly built themselves cabins, furniture, and all the bits and pieces that went to make up a home. At first the woodwork was crude and functional, but pretty soon skillful woodworkers were building the distinctive style of furniture, chests, and boxes that we now call New England colonial.

This little salt box draws its inspiration from a museum piece that was made sometime at the beginning of the seventeenth century. In many ways this box is more than a bit crude—nothing much more than nailed butt joints—but the scrolled braces and the wooden pegs that go to make up the all-wood hinge make it special.

DESIGN, STRUCTURE, AND TECHNIQUE

The box is about $3^3/8$ inches high, 6 inches wide across the span of the lid, and $4^1/2$ inches deep from the front of the lid through to the back (see 3-1 and 3-2).

The charm of this little box lies not in the use of sophisticated joints or exotic woods, but in its qualities of naïveté, boldness, and directness. Okay, so it is a bit of a hammer-and-nails item, but then again, the simple all-wood pin-and-bracket hinges and the wire-brushed texture wonderfully answer the problem of how to build a box without using metal hinges and without worrying about a fragile finish. Or to put it another way, what better way to make a salt box, when salt corrodes just about everything but wood?

WOOD AND MATERIALS

This box needs to be made from a good piece of strong-grained pitch pine. Pitch pine is now a bit scarce, however, but we have discovered that old salvaged pitch pine floorboards are in plentiful supply in many large cities.

For this project you need the following:
- One $7/8$-inch-thick board at 6 inches wide and about 24 inches long for the whole box. (Note that this length allows for a generous amount of cutting waste.)
- Brass or copper nails.
- Beeswax furniture polish.
- PVA glue.

SUGGESTED TOOLS AND SUPPLIES
- A small band saw or a tenon saw.
- A small scroll saw.
- A pencil, ruler, and pair of dividers.

Fig. 3-1. Working drawing, top, *at a grid scale of 2 squares to 1 inch and* bottom, *4 squares to 1 inch. Note how the back top edge needs to be rounded so that the lid opens freely.*

Fig. 3-2. Cutting guide, at a grid scale of 2 squares to 1 inch. Cut the bottom piece to fit the finished box.

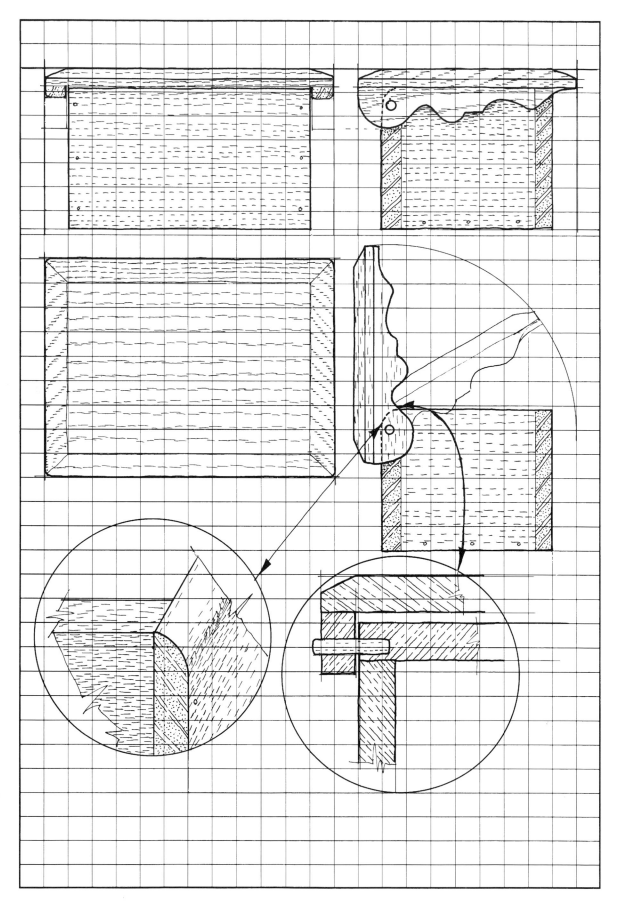

Fig. 3-1

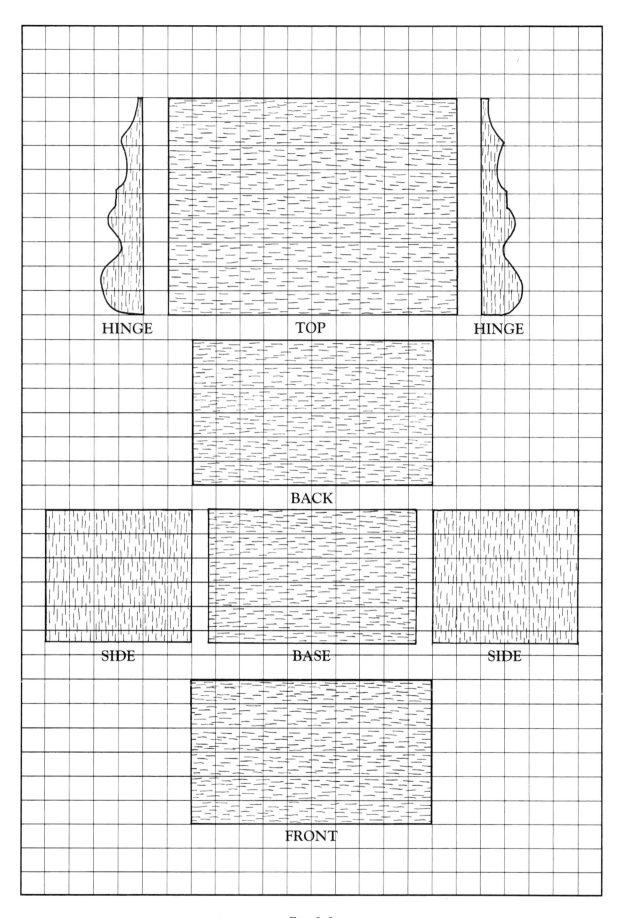

Fig. 3-2

Fig. 3-3. The success of this little box hinges on all the edges and ends being cut true and square.

Fig. 3-5. The pins enable you to fret out two identical profiles without the wood sliding about.

Fig. 3-4. Work at a low sliding angle to the run of the grain. It's best to use a low-angle block plane, as shown.

- An adjustable angle square.
- A good sharp knife for shaping the curves (we use a Swedish sloyd knife).
- A bench plane.
- A small block plane.
- A sheet of graph paper.
- A sheet of tracing paper.
- A hand drill with a 1/4-inch Forstner bit.
- A wire brush.
- All the usual workshop tools and materials, such as sandpaper and scissors.

CONSTRUCTION
Layout and Planing

1. First, familiarize yourself with the project. Take a good long look at the project photographs (see color section) and working drawings (see 3-1 and 3-2). Note how we have deviated slightly from the original in that we have put the whole box together with glue and brass nails rather than wooden pegs. We stay with the wooden pegs for the hinges, however.

2. When you have a clear understanding of the project, check your wood over carefully for potential problems. If it's new, make sure it isn't split. If you're using old wood, like sal-

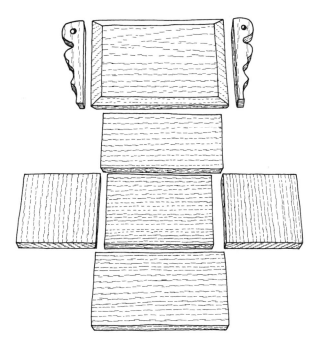

Fig. 3-6. The component parts.

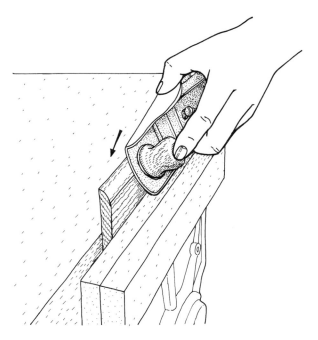

Fig. 3-7. Use the block plane to round over the back edge. Be very careful not to lower the top edge.

vaged floorboards, make sure it's completely free of nails.

3. Plane the wood down on both sides until the board is about 3/8 to 1/2 inch thick.

4. When you have planed the whole board down to a uniform thickness, use the pencil, ruler, square, and knife to lay out the various dimensions that go to make up the box (see 3-3).

5. Finally, use the band saw or tenon saw to cut the wood down into component parts. Clean up the edges with the block plane.

Making the Lid and Scroll Hinges

1. Take the 6-by-4¹/2-inch piece of wood that you have prepared for the lid, label the best face with a pencil, and then use the ruler, pencil, and square to set out the position and size of the chamfered edge.

2. Run a pencil line around the edges of the board dividing the thickness in half, and then run a 1/2-inch border around the best face.

3. With all the guidelines in place, put the workpiece in the vise and use the block plane to chamfer off the waste. Do the along-grain sides first, and then finish up with the end-grain edges (see 3-4). The best procedure for

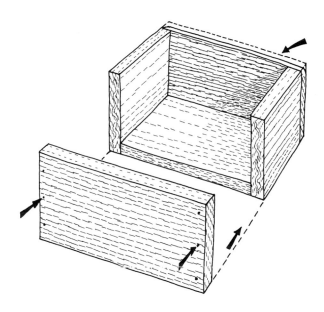

Fig. 3-8. Smear a small amount of glue on mating faces and fix with brass nails. If you are worried about the wood splitting, you can drill pilot holes.

Fig. 3-9. Mark the position of the pivot holes and test the movement of the lid.

Fig. 3-10. Run the pivot holes into the ends of the box.

Fig. 3-11. Glue the pivot pins in place and make sure the lid opens without catching.

planing the end grain of a nice bit of pitch pine is simply to hold the plane at a good angle, and then to work from the end through to the middle.

4. Next, take one of the two little pieces you have set aside for the brackets, and draw the shape of the scroll design on it with a pencil.

5. Position the two pieces of wood together so that the drawn shape is uppermost, and then run a couple of small nails through some part of the waste area. Alternatively, you can use double-sided tape to hold the wood together.

6. Identify the pivot center and run it through with the 1/4-inch Forstner bit. Then use the scroll saw to fret through the double layer, giving you two identical shapes (see 3-5).

Assembly and Finishing

1. Once all eight component parts that go to make the box are completed—lid slab, two

scroll brackets, base, two end boards, and front and back boards—lay them down on the work surface and check them over carefully (see 3-6). Pay particular attention to the run of the grain and to the squareness of the ends. Label all the parts with pencil so that you know what goes where and how.

2. Take the board you have prepared for the back of the box and place it securely in the vise with the back top edge uppermost. Use the block plane to round over the outside box top edge (see 3-7). Aim for a semicircular profile.

3. Take the four box sides and the base and, making sure that the rounded edge is correctly placed and checking the box for squareness, secure them together with glue and brass nails. Use about three nails for each butt joint (see 3-8).

4. Take the lid board and one of the bracket scrolls, and use both of them to establish the precise position of the pivot pins on the ends of the box (see 3-9). Then glue and nail the scroll brackets in place. Test out the action of the lid. If necessary, plane the rounded back edge until the lid opens and closes smoothly.

5. Clamp the lid in place on the box, and then run 1/4-inch-diameter holes through the pivot hole on the bracket and on into the side of the box (see 3-10). Do this for both hinges.

6. Whittle a couple of hinge pegs, and glue them in place. They need to be a tight push-fit in the box itself and a loose, easy fit through the hinges (see 3-11). If necessary, sand them down to fit properly.

7. When you are content with the fit, use the wire brush to take down the areas of soft grain. This is a wonderfully easy procedure—all you do is systematically scrub the brush in the direction of the grain until the hard lines begin to stand out (see 3-12). Pay particular attention to the corners of the box and the side ends of the lid.

8. Finally, give all of the outside faces a coat of beeswax, and burnish the grain to a sheen finish with a stiff brush and a piece of hardwood.

Fig. 3-12. Wire-brush all the surfaces to lower the areas of soft grain. Work in the direction of the grain.

Tips

• If you enjoy box making and would like to speed up the process, consider buying a portable bench surfacer. We have a Ryobi machine—it's a beauty! Just push the rough wood in at one end and smooth, planed wood comes out at the other end—like magic.

• If you enjoy hand planing, you might consider getting a low-angle block plane.

• If you are using old wood, make sure you check it over for old nails and grit before you begin planing.

• It's all too easy to nail the butt joints through the wrong sides. To avoid doing so, it's a good idea to label the mating faces with pencil.

• When you are nailing the back of the box, avoid placing nails near the pivot points.

New England Candle Box

A wall box used traditionally for holding tallow candles and tapers.
Fretted on a scroll saw; shaped with a knife and plane; rabbeted, glued, and nailed;
oiled, waxed, and burnished.

The early American household was very much concerned with candles and tapers—both their use and storage. In homes that were totally dependent on wax candles for nighttime lighting, it was most important that the candles be stored in a place that was both safe and convenient. What better than to have a box placed on the wall—near the center of the house, but away from the dogs and children? Later, when people switched over to oil lamps, such boxes served very nicely for storing tapers, spills, spare wicks, and mantles.

This particular box, with its rabbeted joints and curved front, draws its inspiration from a wall box that was made in the mid-eighteenth century.

DESIGN, STRUCTURE, AND TECHNIQUE

The box measures about 17 inches high from the base to the top of the peaked back board, 12 inches wide, and 4 inches deep (see 4-1 and 4-2).

Note that the grain runs horizontally on the front and side boards and vertically on the back board. We used 6-inch-wide boards throughout, and butt-jointed and glued two pieces for the back board, and cut them down for the box front and sides. The two-piece back board is a bit clumsy, but then again it is true to the spirit of the old-time woodworkers, who were known for their ingenious make-do-and-mend techniques.

Take a good long look at the various drawings and photographs. Note the primary fea-

tures: the symmetrical back board, the beautiful symmetrical cyma curve at the top edge of the front board, and the rabbeted corner joints. The front and back boards have been knife worked to a delicate tapered finish, lifting this box above the ordinary.

Although we used a Stanley duplex rabbet plane (No. 078)—a plane with a depth gauge and an adjustable fence—for cutting the rabbets, you could use just about any small plane with a cutting iron that is as wide as the sole.

WOOD AND MATERIALS

Although this project is best worked in a dense-grained wood like cherry, maple, sycamore, birch, or beech, we used straight-grained cedar. The grain is a bit soft, and you have to be careful about the wood splitting, but the color and working characteristic are excellent. As we were a bit short of wood, we used 6-inch-wide boards, with the base being made from a scrap piece of yellow pine.

Fig. 4-1. Working drawings, at a grid scale of 2 squares to 1 inch. Note the very simple box construction, with the rabbeted front and back boards and the inset base board, all put together with glue and nails.

Fig. 4-2. Cutting guide, at a grid scale of 2 squares to 1 inch. Make the bottom last and cut to fit the finished box.

25

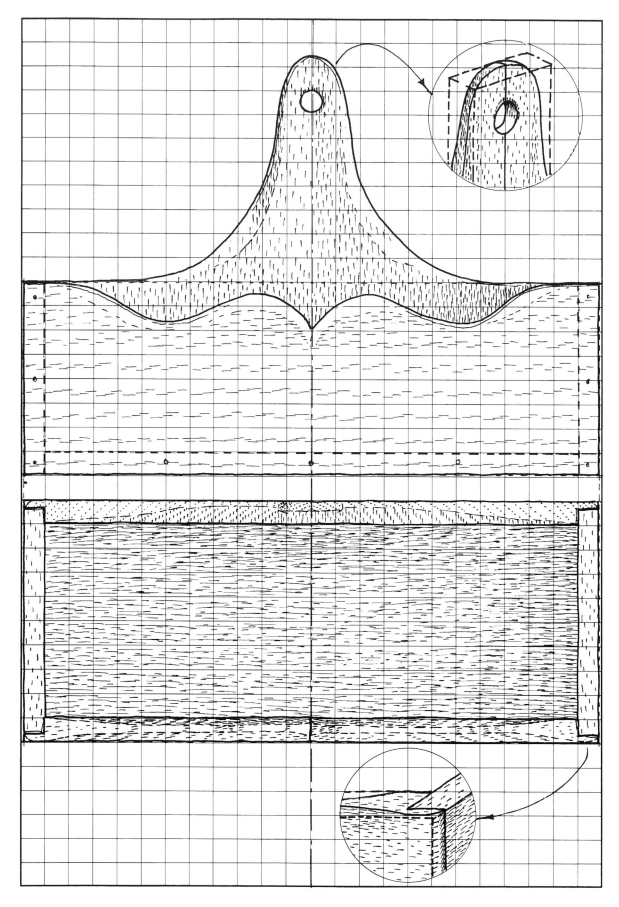

Fig. 4-1

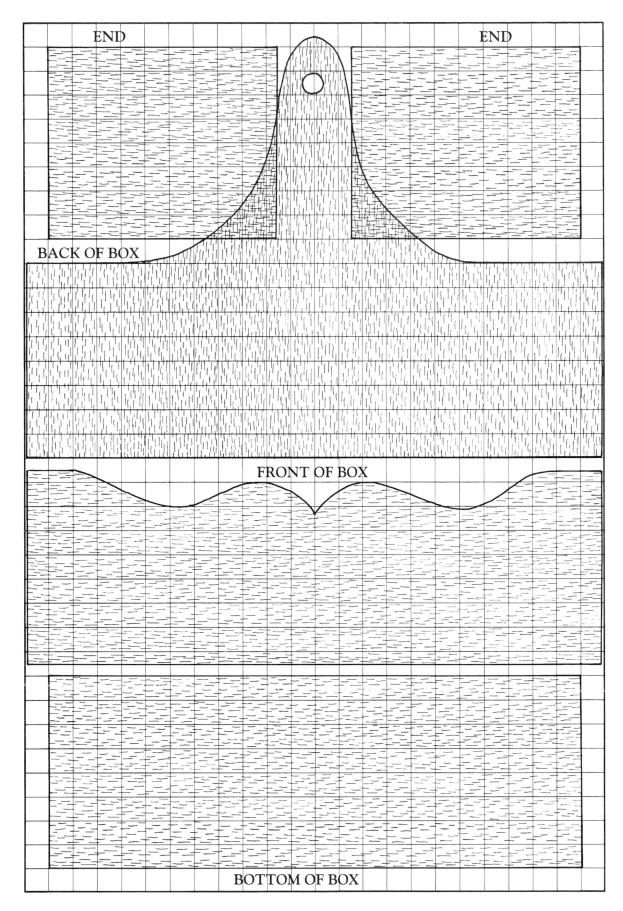

Fig. 4-2

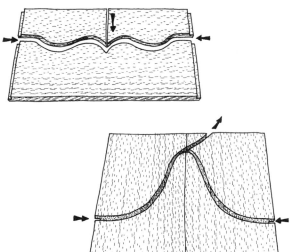

Fig. 4-3. *When working the rabbets, push the fence of the plane hard up against the workpiece, make a series of small dragging strokes so that the spur scores the wood, and then make the through stroke. Although the spur is primarily used for cutting across end grain, we use it for most cuts.*

Fig. 4-5. *Top, to fret out the box front, first run a straight cut to the point of the valley, then follow up with two side-to-center cuts. It's important that the cyma curves be smooth and clean. Bottom, to fret out the box back, make two cuts that run in from the side through to the center. Make sure that the cuts cross the rabbets at a right angle.*

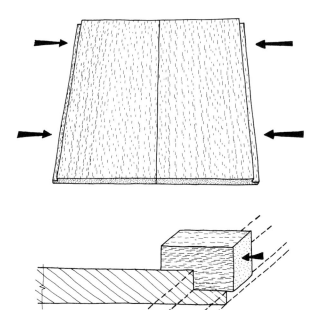

Fig. 4-4. *Top, evenly space the clamps—see the arrows for guidance. Bottom, to avoid stress damage on the thin rabbeted edge, make small clamping blocks to slide between the clamps and the workpiece. You can make these blocks by running a rabbet along a length of wood, and then cutting it into shorter pieces.*

For this project you need the following:
- Two 1/2-inch-thick boards at 9 inches long and 6 inches wide for the back board.
- A 1/2-inch-thick piece at 121/2 inches long and 41/2 inches wide for the front board.
- Two 1/2-inch-thick pieces at 5 inches long and 41/2 inches wide for the sides.
- A 1/2-inch-thick piece at 11 by 4 inches for the base slab.
- Nails.
- Teak oil.
- Beeswax polish.

SUGGESTED TOOLS AND SUPPLIES
- A small bench band saw.
- An electric scroll saw.
- A bench drill press (we use a Delta).
- A 3/8-inch-diameter Forstner drill bit.
- A pencil, ruler, and compass.
- An adjustable angle square.
- A good sharp knife for shaping the curves (we use a Swedish sloyd knife).
- A small block plane.
- A duplex rabbet plane.

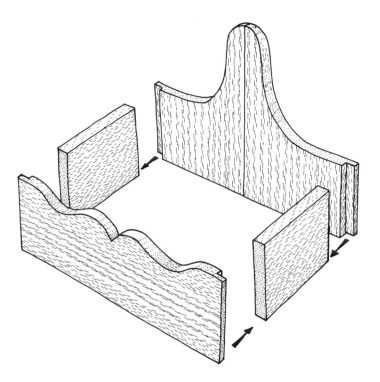

Fig. 4-6. Test-fit the pieces to make sure that the box is square and all the joints are snug, and then use the block plane, knife, and sandpaper to trim to a good finish.

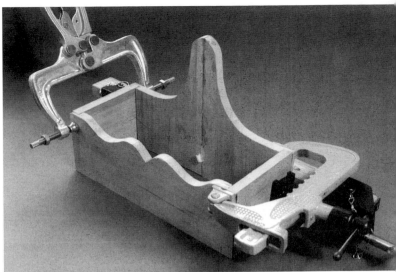

Fig. 4-7. When gluing up, use one clamp to hold the ends in place, and two to hold the front and back boards square. Tighten and adjust the pressure so that the corners are true.

- Hammer.
- A sheet of graph paper.
- A sheet of tracing paper.
- A sheet of thin cardboard for the templates.
- All the usual workshop tools and materials, such as 80-120 grit sandpaper, dividers, and scissors.

CONSTRUCTION

Making the Templates and Laying Out

1. Study the project photographs (see color section) and the working drawings (see 4-1 and 4-2), then draw the designs up to full size and make cardboard templates of the front and back boards.

2. Note how the direction of the grain needs to run through the various boards, and decide whether to make your back board from two boards or a single board.

3. When you have a clear understanding of the project and have selected your wood, use the pencil, ruler, square, and templates to lay out the design on the wood.

Planing the Rabbets

1. Cut the wood to size and square up the faces and edges. If you are using two pieces of wood to make up the back board, label them with pencil so that you know what goes where.

2. Set the fence on your rabbet plane to the thickness of your wood (ours is $1/2$ inch) and set the depth stop to about $2/3$ the thickness of your stock.

3. With the workpiece clamped securely to the bench, and with the plane blade set to make the finest cut, hold the plane level so that the fence is pressed firmly against the workpiece and take a steady, even stroke (see 4-3). Repeat the procedure until the plane ceases to cut shavings. Repeat this step for both back board rabbets.

4. When rabbeting the front board, you will be cutting across the grain, so have the spur down (see Woodshop Techniques section). Start the procedure by dragging the plane a couple of times across the workpiece so that the spur cuts through the grain, and then proceed as already described.

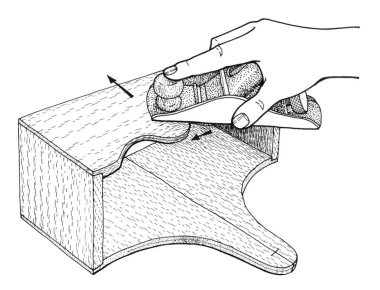

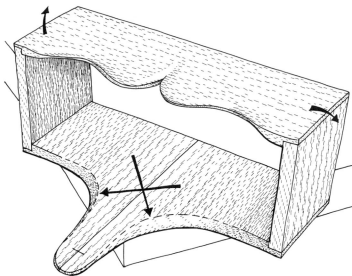

Fig. 4-8. Use a low-angle block plane to model the top edge of the front board. Make a series of sliding skimming strokes, until you achieve a feathered edge.

Fig. 4-9. Hold the box on the edge of the workbench so that the corner supports the back board, and use the block plane to shave down the face edge. Gradually reduce the wood thickness at the peak and top side edges.

5. Finally, take the two back boards, plane them down in width so that they both measure exactly 6 inches wide, and then glue, butt, and clamp so as to make the single 12-inch board width (see 4-4).

Working on the Scroll Saw and Gluing Up

1. Use the templates to draw out the various curves that go to make up the design. Do not lose sight of the fact that the box height at the outside corners and sides needs to finish up at 4 inches.

2. Now use the scroll saw to fret out the double cyma curve of the box front (see 4-5) and the beautiful peak shape of the back board. Be sure that your cuts enter and exit at right angles to the edge of the wood. Work at a nice easy pace, all the while doing your best to make smooth, uninterrupted curves. Run your cuts a little to the waste side of the drawn line, and then cut back to a good finish with the graded sandpaper.

3. Set the five component parts out on the bench and check them over for possible problems. Don't worry too much at this stage

about the precise size of the base board; just make sure that the four sides come together for a good fit (see 4-6). If need be, adjust the rabbets and square off the sawn ends.

4. Test-fit the pieces with clamps, then smear PVA glue on mating faces and clamp up (see 4-7). When clamping, first tighten up the clamps so that they just hold, and check with the square that the sides are true. Then tighten up the clamps until just a little of the glue squeezes out, check again with the square.

5. Wait until the glue has reached the rubbery stage, and then peel off any excess with a knife and chisel.

Shaping and Sanding

1. When the glue has set and the form is stable, remove the clamps. Now comes the exciting task of shaping. If you take a close look at the project picture, you will see that the curved edges have been shaved and rounded to a smooth, sculptural finish so that the various surfaces flow into one another.

2. Run a pencil guideline up and over the

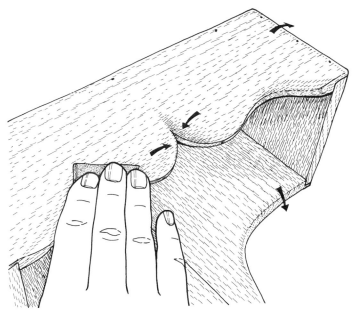

Fig. 4-11. *Use a fold of fine-grade sandpaper to shape and sculpt the top edges and the front of face. Aim for a gently rippled finish at front center. The arrows indicate the run of the curves.*

Fig. 4-10. *Use a joiner's hammer and metal punch to sink the nail heads below the surface of the wood.*

curves to mark the center of the wood thickness. Position the box so that it is on its back with the curves toward your body, and then plane the outside face of the front board at an angle to the grain with a small block plane (see 4-8). It's a beautifully easy procedure, as long as the plane is razor sharp and set at its finest cut. Plane the inside face of the front board in the same manner.

3. Shave down the leading edge of the front board, then repeat the technique for the back board (see 4-9).

4. Also use the block plane to round over the front side edges (see 4-9 and 4-1 bottom detail). Then drill out the hanging hole.

5. Having removed the bulk of the waste with the block plane, now take the knife and gently sculpt the faces of the wood that lead up to the curved edges. The front board needs to be nicely dipped at the center, and the back board peak needs to gently taper up to a beautiful tongue shape (see 4-1 top detail).

Fixing and Finishing

1. When you have achieved a nicely sculpted box, check that it is still square, because you might have twisted it while rounding over the sides. Then cut the base slab to shape, and glue and nail it in place. Nail all the joints, and use a punch to sink the nail heads below the surface of the wood (see 4-10).

2. Take a fold of fine-grade sandpaper and rub the whole works down to a smooth round-edged finish (see 4-11). Don't worry about the usual dictate of trying to keep the lines crisp, just go for a form that looks as if it has been worn and much handled. Sand the

top edges down so that they run in a smooth track around the box.

3. When you are pleased with the quality of the lines and the smoothness of the finish, give the entire piece a couple of thin coats of teak oil and lay it aside to dry.

4. Finally, give the surface another swift rubdown, then apply wax polish and burnish to a high-shine finish.

TIPS

• If you haven't used a rabbet plane before, be sure to practice on scrap wood before starting on the project. This doesn't mean you should try to bully a piece of rough and ragged pine into shape; use a scrap of quality wood to give yourself a fair shot at success.

• It's a good idea to rub candle wax on the side of the fence and the sole of your rabbet plane. The wax protects the plane and makes for easy, friction-free working.

• The rabbet plane's spur and its fixing screw are both tiny and are easily lost, so it's a good idea to always make adjustments over the bench.

• If you are worried that the rabbets on the back boards might become damaged at the clamping stage, you could change the working order and butt-joint the wood before rabbeting.

• When drilling, use a scrap of wood at the back of the workpiece to avoid damage when the bit exits.

• Oily rags can self-combust, so soak them in water before putting them in the trash.

VARIATIONS

• If you do not wish to make rabbeted joints, you can use butt joints and additional nails or small dowel pegs.

• If you want to decorate the piece, you can use a compass and knife to cut a couple of chip-carved hex circles on the front board.

New England Pipe Box

A wall box traditionally used for holding long-stemmed clay churchwarden pipes. Fretted on a scroll saw; shaped with a knife and plane; butt-jointed, glued, and nailed; oiled and burnished.

The early American household was filled with all manner of small wall boxes. There were corner boxes for tallow candles, little shelf boxes for snuffers, elegant boxes for cutlery, boxes for trinkets, boxes for salt, and so on—all made of wood, all put together with minimal joints, and all charming in their naive ingenuity.

This pipe box beautifully illustrates that the New England craftsmen were masters of compass work and the cyma curve. In many ways, wall boxes of this size and type have come to characterize the development of comfortable middle-class life in America in the eighteenth and nineteenth centuries. The overall shape, form, and charm of these small boxes tell us a great deal about the early craftsmen—their creative ability, their skill level, and their inspirations and aspirations.

The low-tech glue-and-nail butt-jointed construction of this box makes it a great project for beginners starting out with a relatively limited tool kit. No problem if you want to make this project but do not smoke long-stemmed clay pipes—you can use the box in the kitchen to hold your wooden spoons and spatulas.

DESIGN, STRUCTURE, AND TECHNIQUE

The box stands about 17 inches high and 6^1/$_2$ inches wide, with a base slab of 5^3/$_4$ by 3^1/$_4$ inches (see 5-1). Note the primary features: the symmetrical back board, the compass-worked and fretted dip-and-arch sequence down the sides of the box, and the cyma curves at the top of the front board. The top ends of the side boards are knife-worked so that they not only run in a smooth curve through to the cyma curves on the front board, but also give the impression that the box edges have been worn.

WOOD AND MATERIALS

This project is best worked in a traditional native American or European hardwood like cherry, maple, sycamore, birch, or beech. Don't be tempted to use an exotic like mahogany—the box will look "overdressed." We have chosen to use cherry throughout. All dimensions are slightly oversize to allow for a small amount of cutting waste.

For this project you need the following:
- A ^{3}/$_8$-inch-thick piece at 18 inches long and 7 inches wide for the back board.
- Two ^{3}/$_8$-inch-thick pieces at 12 inches long and 2^1/$_2$ inches wide for the sides.
- A 6-by-3^1/$_2$-inch piece for the base slab.

Fig. 5-1. Working drawing, at a grid scale of 2 squares to 1 inch. The edge profile is achieved by a simple compass technique, with all the circles being centered on the same line.

Fig. 5-2. Cutting guide, at a grid scale of 2 squares to 1 inch.

Fig. 5-3. Cutting guide, at a grid scale of 2 squares to 1 inch.

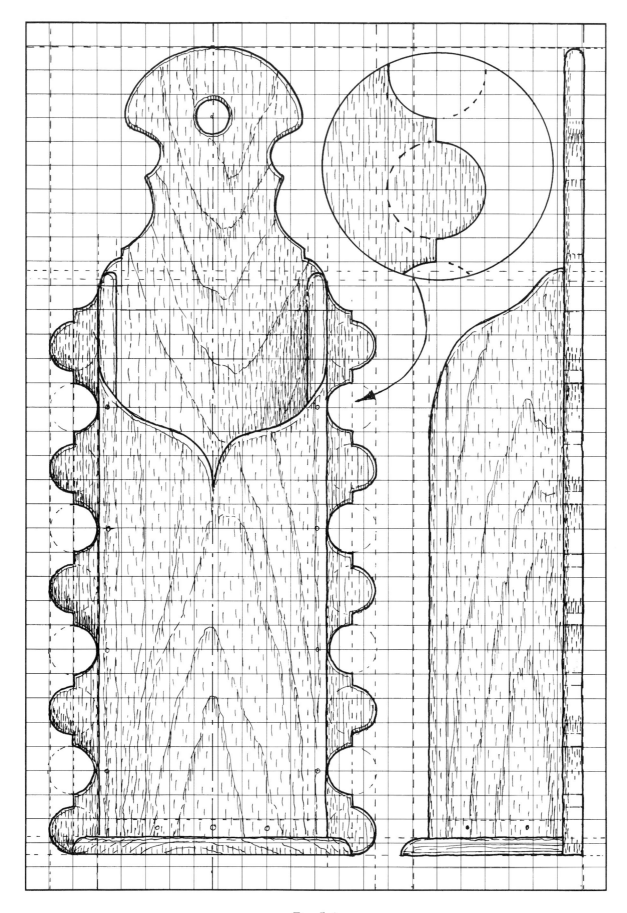

Fig. 5-1

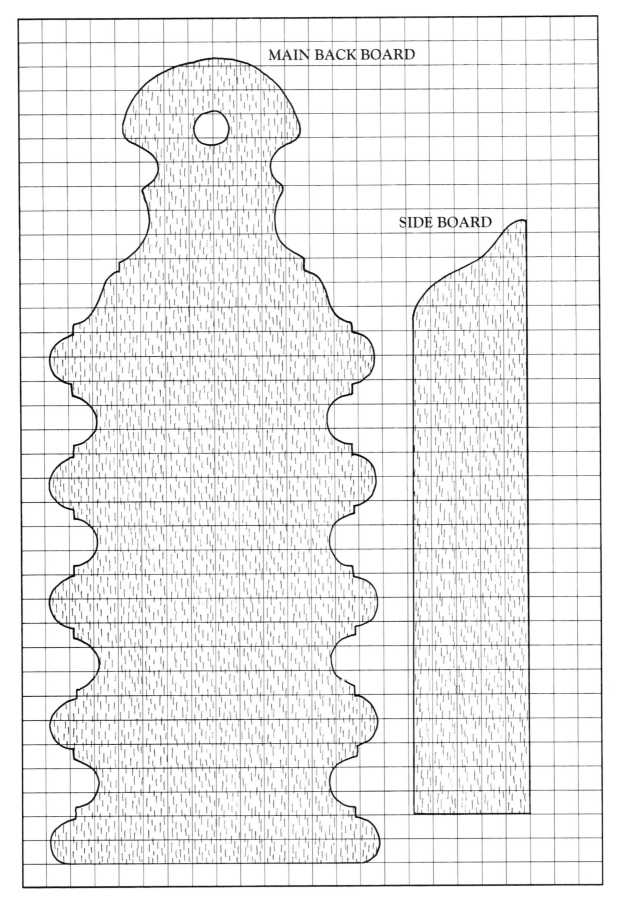

MAIN BACK BOARD

SIDE BOARD

Fig. 5-2

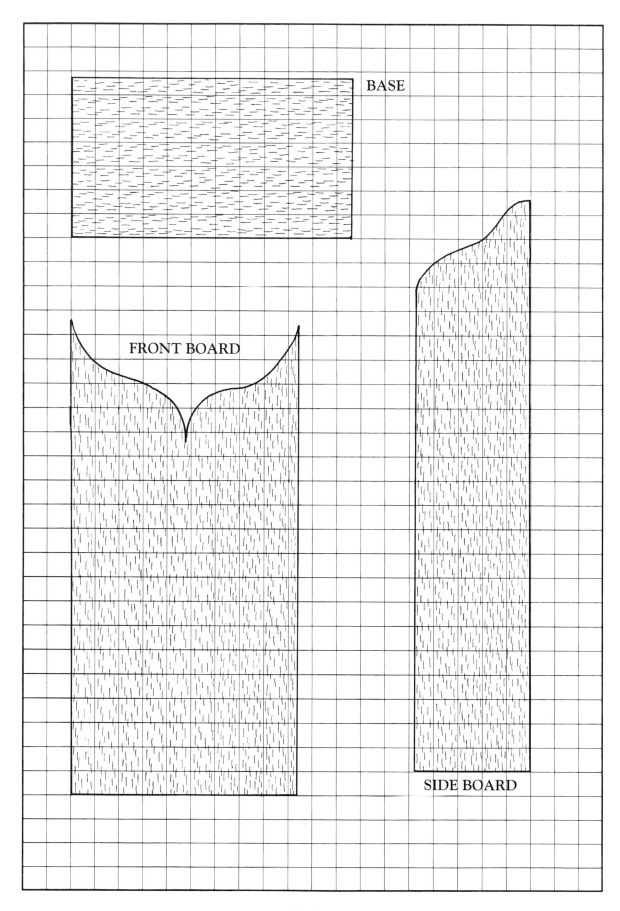

BASE

FRONT BOARD

SIDE BOARD

Fig. 5-3

- A 4-by-2¹/2-inch scrap for the inside-box base piece.
- Nails.
- Linseed oil.
- PVA glue.

SUGGESTED TOOLS AND SUPPLIES
- An electric scroll saw.
- A bench drill press (we use a Delta).
- A ⁵/8-inch-diameter Forstner drill bit.
- A pencil, ruler, and compass.
- An adjustable angle square.
- A good, sharp knife for shaping the curves (we use a Swedish sloyd knife).
- A small block plane.
- A sheet of graph paper.
- A sheet of tracing paper.
- A sheet of thin cardboard, such as a cereal box, for the template.
- A joiner's hammer.
- A punch.
- All the usual workshop tools and materials, such as sandpaper, dividers, and scissors.

CONSTRUCTION
Making Templates and Laying Out

1. Study the project photographs (see color section) and working drawings (see 5-1, 5-2, and 5-3), and gather all your tools and materials. Then use the pencil, square, and ruler to set out the primary rectangles—the back board, front board, and one side board—on the sheet of cardboard. Don't worry about the curves at this stage; just make sure that all the forms are true and square.

2. Now use the pencil, ruler, and compass to lay out all the curves that go to make up the design. First study the working drawing details (see 5-1 top) and consider how the characteristic edge profile can easily be drawn out with a compass and ruler. Note the circle radius of ¹/2 inch and the between-circle step-off of ¹/4 inch.

3. Doublecheck that all the lines are drawn correctly, then use a small pair of fine-point scissors to cut out the template profile. Try to achieve a crisp line (see 5-4).

4. Using the cardboard templates, lay out the designs on the best face of the wood.

Fig. 5-4. Use a small pair of scissors to cut out the template profile from a piece of thin cardboard.

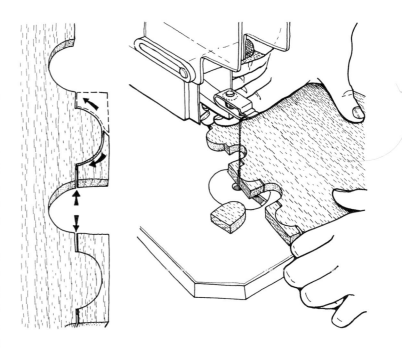

Fig. 5-5. Left, *the sequence of cuts is to first remove the* U *shapes, then cut the little steps, and finally clear the arch by cutting from the center toward first one side, then the other. Right, clear the arch one side at a time. Note that the guard is raised in this illustration so that you have a clear view of the cut being made. You should always work with the guard in place, however.*

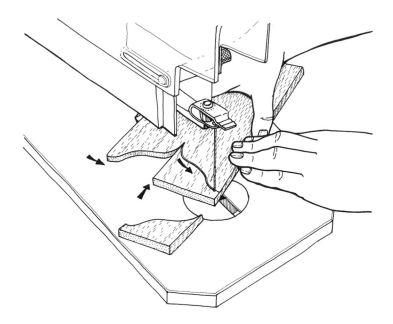

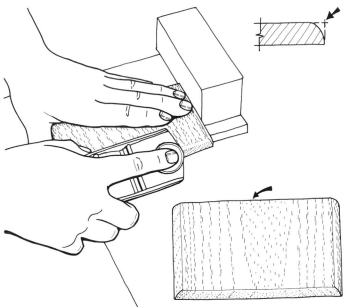

Fig. 5-6. To cut the box front profile, first cut a straight line down to the center point, and then follow along the curves so that the waste falls away in two pieces.

Fig. 5-8. Left, *hold the base in the bench hook sawing jig and use the block plane to round over the sharp edges.* Top right, *cross section showing the shape of the bevel.* Bottom right, *leave the back edge square.*

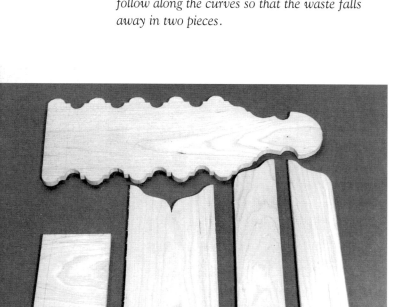

Fig. 5-7. *The five outer edge components, as they come from the saw.*

Working on the Scroll Saw

1. Now comes the pleasuresome task of working on the scroll saw. Fit a new blade—the finer the better. The blade needs to be set with the teeth pointing downward toward the floor so that they cut on the down stroke. Check that the tension is correct; the blade should ping when plucked. Always remember to slacken the blade off after use. If you don't have a scroll saw, you can use a hand tool like a fret or coping saw.

2. Keeping in mind that it's not so easy to change the direction of a continuous cut, the simplest procedure is to first cut all of the U shapes, then run an in-and-out cut on each of the little 1/4-inch steps, and finally clear each arch with two cuts. Working in this way ensures a smooth, crisp profile (see 5-5).

3. Fret out the box front profile by running the first cut down into the sharp peak, straight in and out, and then clearing the waste with a single cut that runs in along one curve and out along the other (see 5-6). If you have done it right, the waste will fall way in two pieces.

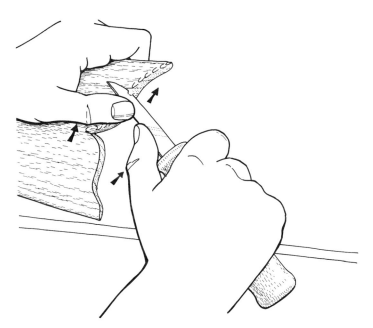

Fig. 5-9. Use the knife to shave the edge down to a good finish. Work with a tight, thumb-braced action, with your elbows tucked into your waist.

Fig. 5-10. To round over each of the U shapes, use a fold of sandpaper and work with a slight rolling action. If you wish, you can wrap the sandpaper around a fat dowel.

4. Now fret out the two side boards and the base slab. It's all pretty straightforward; just be sure to run your lines of cut slightly to the waste side of the drawn lines.

Shaping

1. When you have your five component parts—the base slab, back board, front board, and two sides (see 5-7)—test-fit the pieces to make sure that you have cut all of the parts correctly. Note that the inner base piece is cut out at a later stage to make sure that it is an accurate fit.

2. To shape the base board, first label the front and two side edges with pencil, and then use the block plane to round over what will be the top edges of the front and sides. Do not round over the back edge. The easiest procedure is to butt the workpiece firmly against the bench hook and then go at it nice and easy (see 5-8). Be careful when you are planing the end-grain front edge that you don't split off the side grain at the corners. It's best to trim the side edges first, then tackle the end-grain front edge.

Fig. 5-11. The side boards need to fit snugly against the inside-box base piece. Make sure that the top of the side board is correctly aligned. If need be, clamp a block of waste wood to the inside of the box to help you keep everything square.

Fig. 5-12. It's all too easy for a butt-jointed box to get pushed out of square, so be sure to check for squareness before and after gluing and nailing.

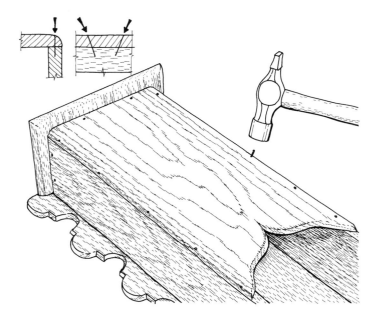

Fig. 5-13. Top left detail, *drive the nails in at a slightly skewed angle so as to create "dovetails."* Bottom, *drive the nails in at the corners, and then fill in as you think fit. If you are worried about the wood splitting, drill pilot holes before nailing.*

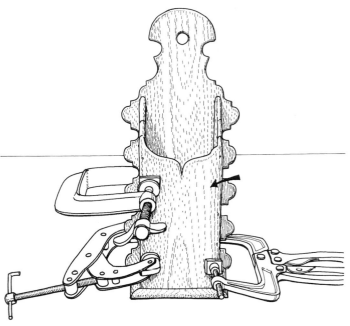

Fig. 5-14. *Set the clamps in place, with blocks of waste between the metal heads and the work-piece, and then gradually tighten up. As you do so, check with a square every now and then that all is correct.*

3. To shape the box front, use the knife to skim away the corners from the curved edge. Shave the front face down so that the edge is reduced to a slender thickness of about 1/4 inch. Aim for an edge that feathers out to a smooth, rolled curve. Hold the knife with a two-handed, thumb-braced cut, and work from the center to side (see 5-9).

4. To shape the dip-and-arch edge, first use the knife to swiftly skim off the sharp edges, then use a fold of fine-grade sandpaper to rub the edges down to a smooth finish. The best procedure is to first rub each of the dips in a downward direction, and then rub the whole edge down to a slightly feathered, smooth fin-ish (see 5-10).

5. Now cut the small base block to fit inside the box, and bring to a good finish.

Assembly and Finishing

1. Test-fit all of the cut and shaped pieces. When you are happy with the overall fit and

finish, label the parts with pencil so that you know what goes where and how, and mark areas that need to be glued. Draw in as many guidelines as you think necessary.

2. Glue and nail the two base slabs together, then smear glue on mating edges and set the base in place on the back board. Next, smear glue on mating edges of one side board and set it in place against the back and the base (see 5-11).

3. Glue and position the other side board, and make sure everything is true and square. Nail through from the side, the underside of the base, and the back (see 5-12).

4. Smear glue on all mating faces of the box front and set it in place. Secure it with nails (see 5-13). Use the punch to drive the nail heads below the surface.

5. When you are happy with the arrangement, clamp it up (see 5-14) and lay it aside until the glue has set. If you don't have clamps, you could use a binding of twine and a twist stick.

6. When the glue is dry, remove the clamps. Trim and shape the top edge of the box front so that it runs smoothly into the side boards. Give the whole works a final rubdown with the finest grade of sandpaper.

7. Clean away all dust and debris, then brush on two thin coats of linseed oil. First apply one coat and let it dry, give the entire piece a swift sanding, then lay on the second coat.

8. Finally, give all the surfaces another sanding, wipe away the dust, and use the beeswax polish to burnish all the surfaces to a deep sheen finish.

TIP

• After you have made your templates, if you are worried that one of the parts is too small, concentrate your efforts on the back board, and then cut the other parts to fit.

Early American Candle Box

A hanging wall box used traditionally for holding candles.
Fretted on a scroll saw; shaped with a knife and plane; rabbeted and grooved;
glued and nailed; beeswaxed and burnished.

Boxes of this type, size, and character tended to be used for holding candles. The box would be hung on the wall—usually by the fire or at the bottom of the stairs—so that when the householders wended their weary way to bed, the candles were conveniently at hand. The design is such that the box can be left in place on the wall and opened by sliding the lid upward, or the box can be removed with one hand while the lid is slid back with the other. Either way, the design of the lid allows the candles to be stored and removed without damaging the wicks. And if, as often happened, the box had to be negotiated in the dark, it could be opened without worrying about hinges, locks, or catches.

Our box draws its inspiration from a museum original that was made of mahogany sometime in the first quarter of the nineteenth century.

DESIGN, STRUCTURE, AND TECHNIQUE

The box is about 14½ inches high, 4 inches wide, and 3½ inches deep, with the base measuring 4 by 3½ inches (see 6-1 and 6-2). Note that the single 3½-inch-wide board, which goes to make the sides, base, and top, is first grooved before being cut into four pieces and then variously rabbeted and sized.

If you are a beginner, rest assured that this is one of the least complicated projects in the book. If you can use a rabbet plane and a plough, or a multiplane, the making stages are wonderfully simple and direct.

WOOD AND MATERIALS

Though the museum original box is made from mahogany, we favor using renewable wood types and have chosen to use plum throughout. If you have trouble finding plum, you could use cherry or even a well-seasoned piece of pencil cedar.

For this project you need the following:
- A ⅜-inch-thick piece at 36 inches long and 4 inches wide for the side boards, top end, and base.
- A ¼-inch-thick piece at 30 inches long and 4 inches wide for the front and back boards.
- Beeswax polish.
- Brass dome-head nails.

SUGGESTED TOOLS AND SUPPLIES
- A workbench with a vise and holdfast.
- An electric scroll saw.
- A bench drill press (we use a Delta).
- A ⅜-inch-diameter Forstner drill bit.
- A pencil, ruler, and compass.
- PVA glue.
- An adjustable angle square.
- A good sharp knife for shaping the curves (we use a Swedish sloyd knife).

Fig. 6-1. Working drawing, at a grid scale of 2 squares to 1 inch. Front view, side view, and plan cross section.

Fig. 6-2. Cutting guide, at a grid scale of 2 squares to 1 inch.

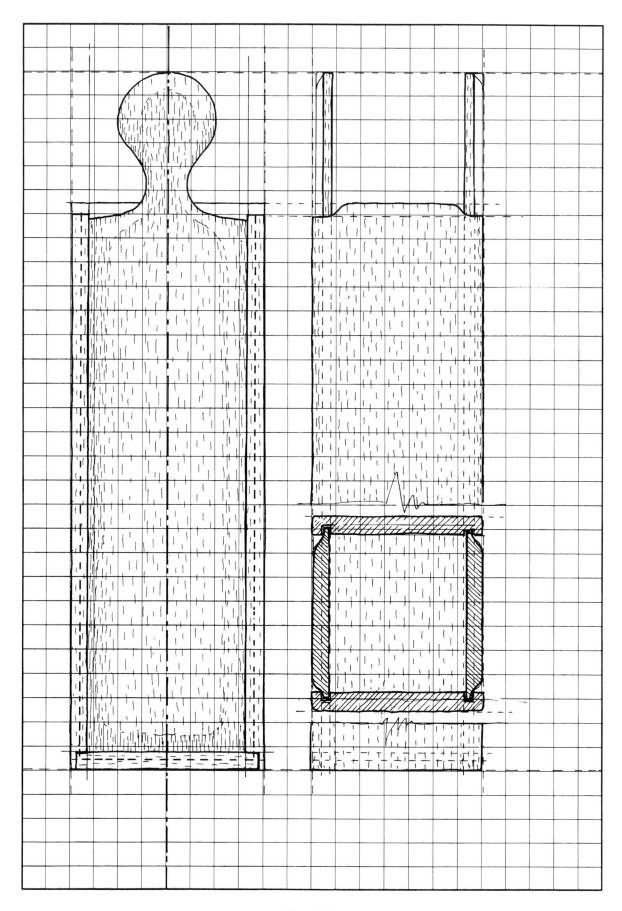

Fig. 6-1

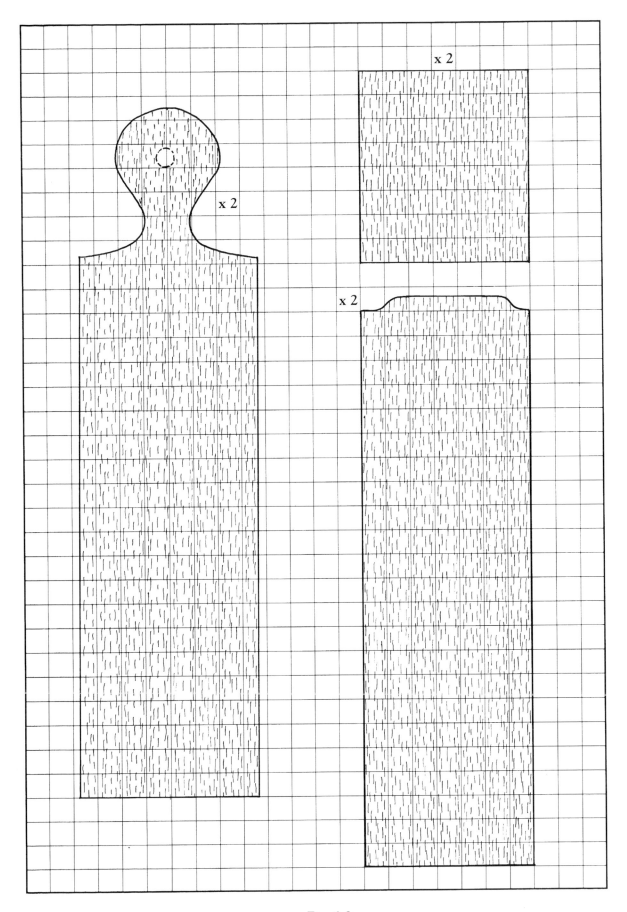

Fig. 6-2

Fig. 6-3. Use your fingertips to check that the fence is held true and square against the wood.

Fig. 6-5. Use a clamp and a bench stop to secure the wood while you are working. Note how we use a piece of wood in the vise for the stop.

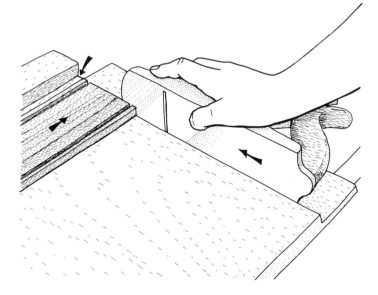

Fig. 6-4. Place a waste piece at the far corner, against the shooting board stop, and run the plane on its side. Make sure that the workpiece is butted up firmly against the stop.

• A shooting board or shooting bench hook.
• A plough or multiplane with a ³⁄₁₆-inch-wide blade for cutting the grooves.
• A rabbet plane (we use a Stanley duplex).
• A bench plane.
• A small block plane.
• A sheet of graph paper.
• A sheet of tracing paper.
• A variety of clamps.
• A small hand drill with a bit that is slightly smaller than the diameter of the brass nails.
• All the usual workshop tools and materials, such as sandpaper, dividers, and scissors.

CONSTRUCTION
Preparing the Wood and Laying Out
1. Study the project photographs (see color section) and the working drawings (see 6-1), then check your wood over for potential problems. The grooves and rabbets all need to be crisply worked, so avoid wood that is knotty or coarse grained.

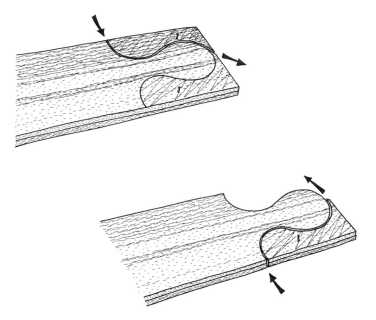

Fig. 6-6. Top, *shade in the areas of waste. Then saw on the waste side of the drawn line—in at one shoulder and out at the head.* Bottom, *repeat the procedure for the other side of the shape.*

Fig. 6-7. *Use the block plane to skim the side and bottom edges to a thickness of about 1/8 inch.*

2. Take the 36-inch-long board that you have chosen for the box sides, base, and top, and plane it down to a finished size of 3 1/2 inches wide and 3/8 inch thick.

3. Take the piece of wood that you have chosen for the front and back boards, and plane it down to a finished size of 3 1/2 inches wide and just a shade under 1/4 inch thick.

4. Select what you consider to be the best faces of the wood, and then use a pencil to mark the opposite faces of the wood on the "inside."

5. Finally, use the pencil, ruler, and square to lay out all the measurements that go to make up the design—the lengths of the various pieces, and the positions of the grooves and rabbets. Be sure to draw all the lines on the inside face.

Ploughing the Grooves and Cutting to Size

1. Now take the 3/8-inch-thick board and clamp it down on the bench so that the inside face is uppermost.

2. Take your plough or multiplane (we use

a Stanley 45) and adjust the fence and depth stop so that the 3/16-inch-wide blade is set up to make a 3/16-inch-deep groove about 3/16 inch in from the edge of the board.

3. Make a trial run with the plane on a piece of scrap wood, then run the plane firmly alongside the workpiece to cut the 3/16-by-3/16-inch square groove. The best approach is to make a series of very light cuts, all the while holding the plane in such a way that your fingertips keep the fence square and true (see 6-3). Repeat the procedure on the opposite edge of the board.

4. Mark out the four lengths with the cutting knife and square, double-check that all is exact, and then use a gents saw to cut the wood to length. You should end up with two boards at 12 inches for the long sides and two short boards at 3 3/4 inches for the top and base.

5. Finally, set the boards one at a time on the shooting board, and use the bench and the block plane to skim the end-grain ends to a smooth, true finish (see 6-4).

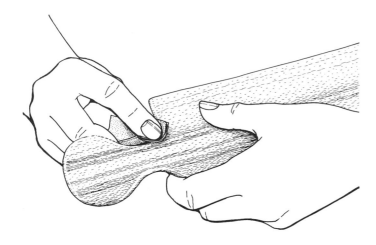

Fig. 6-8. Use a fold of fine-grade sandpaper to finish the edges of the lid.

Fig. 6-10. Test-fit the sides and ends, and test the lid in the slot.

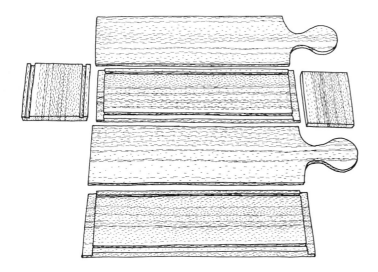

Fig. 6-9. Spread the component parts out on the bench and check them over for size and fit.

Rabbeting the End Joints

1. Take the two long boards and set them side by side on the bench so that two ends overlap the bench vise by about 1½ inches. Secure the boards with the holdfast and a stop, and make sure that everything will stay put. Clamp a small scrap piece firmly alongside the furthermost board to prevent split-off when the plane comes to the end of its run (see 6-5).

2. Set the rabbet plane so that the fence and the depth stop allow for a rabbet step that is about ¼ inch deep and ⅜ inch wide.

3. When you are happy with the bench and plane setup—and this may well take considerable time to get right—run the rabbets across both ends of both long boards (see 6-5).

Making the Lid and Back Board

1. First draw the lid design up to scale and make a tracing, then pencil press-transfer the lines through to the best face of the lid board.

2. Align all the edges of the front and back boards and nail them together, placing the nails in the areas of waste. Use the scroll saw to fret out the shape of the tonguelike handle. Work at a steady, even pace, all the while

making sure that the line of cut is slightly to the waste side of the drawn line (see 6-6).

3. With the front board butted against the bench stop so that the best face is uppermost, take the block plane and skim the side and bottom edges down to a thickness of about 1/8 inch (see 6-7). Aim for a smooth-curved, convex cross section, with the feathered edges fitting easily in the grooves. Repeat the same procedure with the back board, only this time aim for a tight push-fit in the grooves.

4. Finally, use the knife and sandpaper to model the handles on both boards down to a smooth, round-edged finish (see 6-8).

Fitting and Finishing

1. Take the small top end board and use the plane to swiftly cut the wood down to the level of the groove. Do this on both edges.

2. Spread all of the pieces out on the work surface and check them over for size and finish (see 6-9). Label all the boards with pencil so that you know precisely how they relate one to another.

3. Test-fit the pieces to see how they all come together (see 6-10). If necessary, adjust the depth of the rabbets or the width of the back and front boards. Drill and sand the hole in the back board handle.

4. Take the top end board and use the block plane and knife to round over the front and back edges. Aim for a top that is convex as seen from the side view, with the curve being cut back so that it is flush with the grooves. Then use the knife to shape the side boards so that the top edge profile follows the curved top end board (see 6-11).

5. Test-fit to make sure the corner joints come together flush and square, then smear PVA glue on the mating faces of the joints and on the edges of the back board, and lightly clamp up. Check the corners with the square, and if necessary, adjust the pressure or position of the clamps. Use a knife to clean up the profile (see 6-12).

6. While the glue is setting, look at the project picture and see how we have followed the spirit of the American folk-art tradition by personalizing the box lid with initials and

Fig. 6-11. *Carve the sides to follow the shape of the curved-section top board.*

Fig. 6-12. *While the clamps are still in place, use the knife to put the final touches to the edge profile.*

a motif. We have chosen to set our initials and a heart, but you could use a meaningful date, a whole name, or whatever.

7. When the glue is dry, transfer your chosen design onto the best face of the lid. The safest procedure for applying the decorative nails is to first make pilot holes with the hand drill and small bit. Cover your motif with holes that are slightly smaller than the nails and run through the thickness of the wood. Clip the nails to length, dip them in glue, and then tap them in place. Don't be tempted to simply hammer in the brass nails. If you do, the dense grouping of the nails is likely to split the wood.

8. Finally, rub the whole works down to a smooth finish with a fine-grit sandpaper and clean away the dust. Then wipe all the surfaces over with beeswax, and burnish to a dull sheen finish. If you are using brassed-steel nails, rather than solid brass nails, then sand before nailing.

TIPS

• To prevent the rabbet plane from splitting off short grain as it crosses the ends of the grooves, you can pack the grooves with thin strips of waste wood.

• If you don't have the use of a rabbet plane, you could cut the rabbets with a saw and chisel, or use butt joints instead.

VARIATIONS

• If you prefer, you can use a brush stroke pattern or even calligraphy to decorate your box.

Family Document Box

A box used for holding all the important family papers.
Shaped with a molding plane; butt-jointed; glued and nailed; painted, varnished,
and decorated with gold paint Fraktur-style lettering.

Most early American households had a document or deed box for storing all the important family papers, such as wedding licenses, birth and baptismal certificates, property sale and purchase papers, family letters, and wills. Though just about any strong, sturdy box could be used for the purpose, it was the custom in many communities to purchase or make a box specifically designed for documents. Such boxes were well built, painted in a somber dark color like black, green, or maroon, and decorated with Fraktur-style initials. In many instances these strongboxes were screwed or bolted to some part of the house—for example, to the floor beside the bed—and fitted with a heavy padlock.

DESIGN, STRUCTURE, AND TECHNIQUE

The box stands about 9³/4 inches high and is 17 inches long across the widest part of the molded lid, with the box base measuring 16 by 10 inches (see 7-1 and 7-2). Note the primary features: the chamfered panel base slab that fits into a ploughed groove that runs around the inside of the box, the solid slab lid with beaded edge and raised panel field, and the use of naive Fraktur-style letters. To give this document box an authentic look, we used rather stern, businesslike brass handles and a flipover type catch that takes a padlock.

If you have a combination plane in your tool kit and you like to cut beads and trenches, you will really enjoy making this project. If you don't have access to a combination plane,

you can get away with using a plough plane and a small rabbet plane, plus a gouge.

WOOD AND MATERIALS

This project is best made in a traditional easy-to-work wood like pine or tulip poplar. We used pine for the box sides and tulip for the lid and base. All dimensions are slightly oversize to allow for a small amount of cutting waste.

For this project you need the following:

• A ³/4-inch-thick piece of pine at 60 inches long and 8 inches wide for all the box sides.

• A ¹/2-inch-thick piece of tulip at 16 by 10 inches for the base.

• A 1¹/4-inch-thick piece of tulip at 17 by 11 inches for the lid slab.

• Matte black oil paint, such as blackboard paint.

• Gold paint, the best you can afford.

• Clear yacht or spar varnish.

• Nails.

• PVA glue.

SUGGESTED TOOLS AND SUPPLIES

• A ripsaw.

• A crosscut saw.

• A pencil, ruler, and pair of dividers.

• An adjustable angle square.

• A bench plane.

• A small block plane.

• A combination plane with a ¹/2-inch-diameter bead blade, a ¹/4-inch-wide plough cutter, and a ³/4-inch-wide chisel cutter (we use an old Stanley 45).

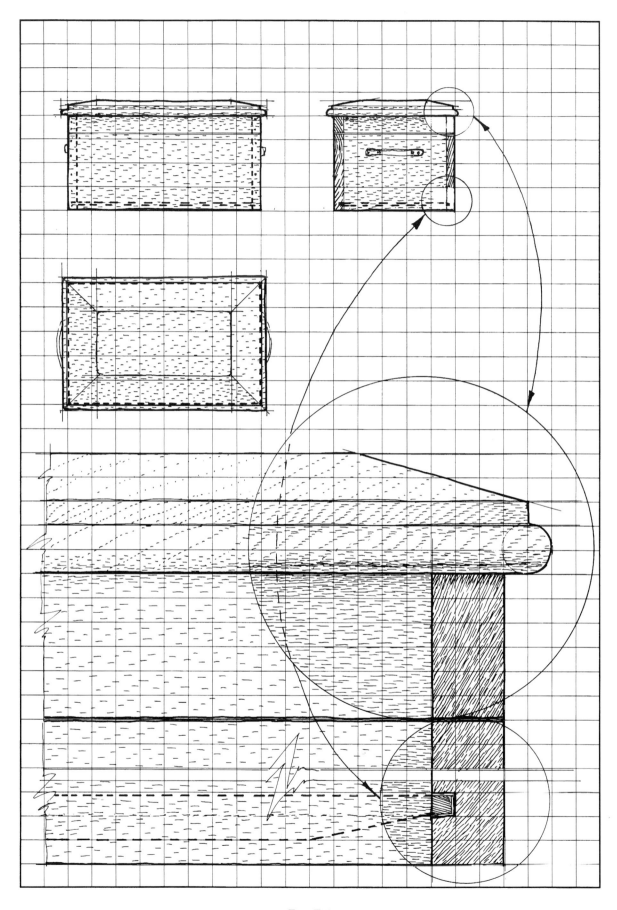

Fig. 7-1

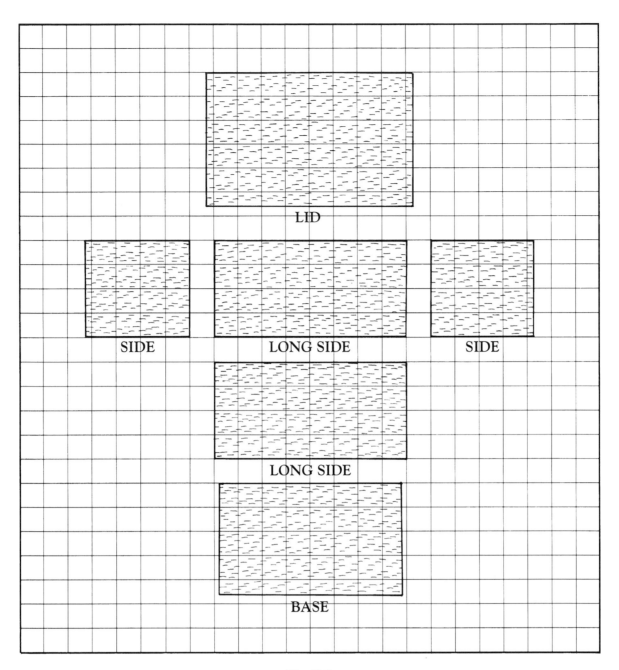

LID

SIDE   LONG SIDE   SIDE

LONG SIDE

BASE

Fig. 7-2

Fig. 7-1. Working drawing, top, at a grid scale of 1 square to 2 inches and bottom, 4 squares to 1 inch. Note especially the solid profile of the lid slab, and the way the base fits in a groove.

Fig. 7-2. Cutting guide, at a grid scale of 1 square to 2 inches.

Fig. 7-3. Decorative frame for the lid design.

Fig. 7-4. Alphabet pattern.

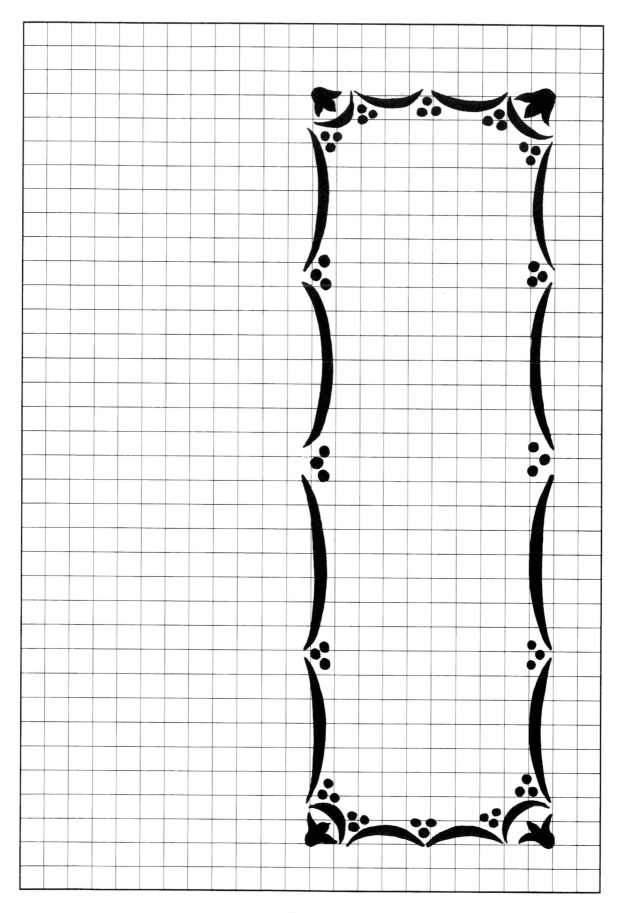

Fig. 7-3

Fig. 7-4

Fig. 7-5. Run the groove along the inside box face board. Gill has taken her left hand away so that you can see the plane in relation to the edge of the board.

Fig. 7-6. Make a series of light passes. Use your left hand to maintain pressure, holding the fence firmly against the side of the board.

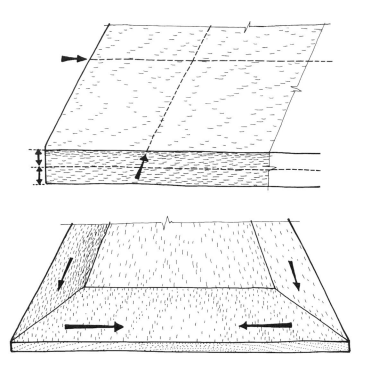

Fig. 7-7. Top, *draw the guideline borders on the base slab so that it is 1 1/2 inches wide, and divide the board thickness in half.* Bottom, *plane in the direction of the arrows, working in the direction of the grain.*

- A sheet of graph paper.
- A sheet of tracing paper.
- A joiner's hammer.
- A punch.
- All the usual workshop tools and materials, such as sandpaper and scissors.

CONSTRUCTION

Making the Sides

1. First study the project picture (see color section) and the working drawings (see 7-1), and get your tools and wood together. Then take the prepared 8-inch-wide board and mark it out and saw it down to make two 60-inch lengths, one 6 1/2 inches wide and the other 1 1/2 inches wide.

2. Clamp with 6 1/2-inch-wide board flat down on the workbench, then fit the combination plane with the 1/4-inch-wide plough or groove cutter, set the fence to 1/2 inch, and run a 1/4-by-1/4-inch groove along the inside box face of the board (see 7-5).

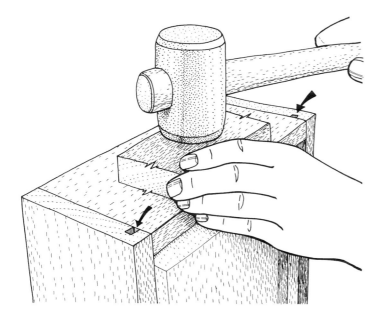

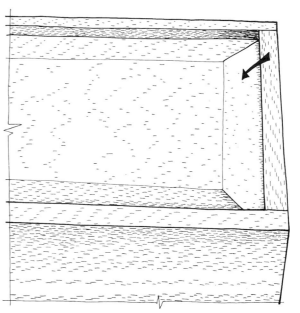

Fig. 7-8. Check that the parts fit. Use a mallet or rubber hammer to tap the parts together. Note that the waste wood has been cut away in the drawing to show the ends of the grooves as noted by the arrows. You will need to fill the groove ends at a later stage.

Fig. 7-9. When you look at the bottom of the box, you should be able to see the chamfered edges of the base board.

3. The secret of success when using the combination plane is to make a light cut, putting most of your effort into holding the fence firmly against the side of the board (see 7-6).

4. After you have cut the 1/4-by-1/4-inch groove, use the pencil and square to mark the board off into two lengths at 16 inches long and two lengths at 6 1/2 inches. Mark off the 1 1/2-inch-wide board in the same way. Check the measurements, then saw the wood down into these eight pieces, which will go to make up the box sides.

Making and Fitting the Base Slab

1. Take the 1/2-inch-thick 16-by-10-inch slab—the piece for the base—and mark it out to 15 by 9 inches. Cut it down, making sure that the corners are true.

2. Use the pencil, ruler, and square to mark off 1 1/2-inch-wide borders and to divide the 1/2-inch thickness in half (see 7-7 top).

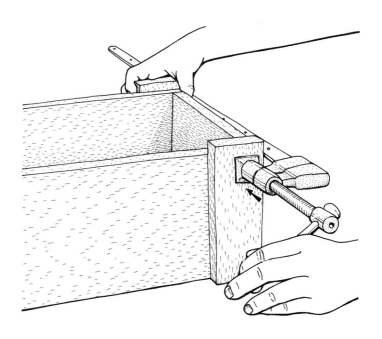

Fig. 7-10. Glue the butt joints and clamp up the box. Check that the sides are square, and then allow the glue to set.

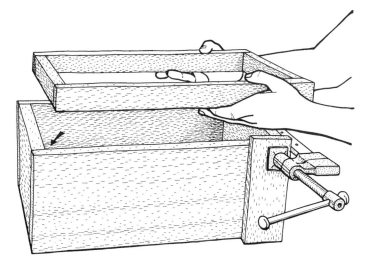

Fig. 7-11. Check that the lid sides are a good fit, and then drive in the nails.

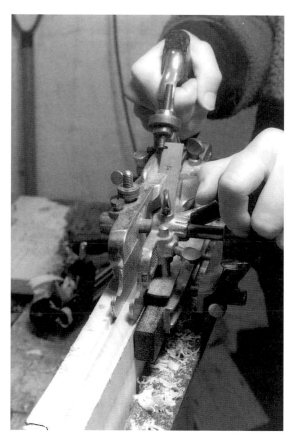

Fig. 7-13. Run a 1/2-inch-diameter bead around the edge of the slab. A piece of scrap wood at the end of the run prevents damage to the short grain edges.

Fig. 7-12. Make sure that the sledge runner is aligned with the side edge of the blade.

3. Secure the workpiece flat down on the bench with the holdfast, and use the bench and block planes to cut away the slopes. The best procedure is to first plane with the grain—along the length of the boards—and then work the ends by planing in from the sides (see 7-7 bottom). Try to achieve clean, straight miters at the corners.

4. Continue skimming down the slopes until the edge of the base slab is a tight push-fit in the ploughed grooves.

5. Having planed all four slopes down to a good finish, so that the edge pushes neatly into the groove, test-fit to check how the box comes together (see 7-8). You might need to tap the sides in place, but in doing so, be careful not to twist the wood or overdo the tap-

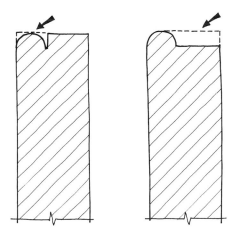

Fig. 7-14. Left, *start by cutting the 1/2-inch diameter half-circle profile.* Right, *clear the waste with the 3/4-inch-wide cutter.*

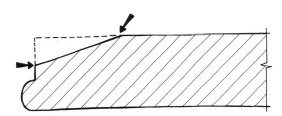

Fig. 7-15. *The slope starts about 1/4 inch above the bead and angles back to a depth of about 1 1/2 inches.*

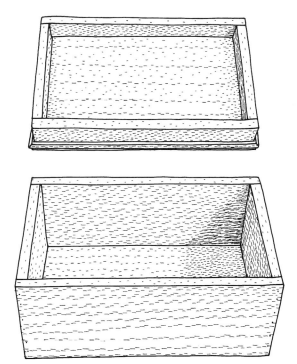

Fig. 7-16. *The assembled lid and box, ready to be fitted with hinges and painted.*

ping. If need be, you can sand one side of the groove for a good fit. Your base slab can be positioned with either side up. We opted to have the side with the sloped edges facing down toward the bottom of the box (see 7-9). While you are at it, plan out how you are going to clamp up.

6. When you are happy with the fit, clear the working area of clutter, then smear glue on the mating faces of the butt joints and clamp up (see 7-10). Don't glue the base slab in the groove—it needs to be able to move.

7. Glue and clamp the lid rim sides in the manner already described. Check the lid rim for a good fit (see 7-11). When the glue is set, hammer nails into the joints and use a punch to drive the heads below the surface.

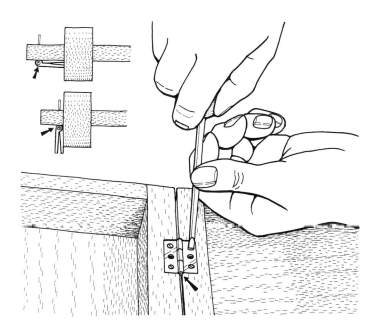

Fig. 7-17. Top left, *use the chosen hinge to get the appropriate marking gouge step-off sizes.* Bottom, *having first drilled pilot holes, the best procedure is to put the outside screws in first, test the fit, and then drive in the center screws. Leave the screw slots all running in the same direction.*

Fig. 7-18. Use a fine-point brush to paint the letters and the decorative frame. Use a slight downward pressure so that the tip spreads and broadens the line.

Making the Lid Slab

1. First make sure that your combination plane is in good working order (see 7-12). Check that the 1/2-inch-diameter bead cutter is honed and fitted, the sledge runners are spaced so that they match up with the blade, and the fence is set so that the bead lines up with one edge (see 7-1, large circle detail). It's always a good idea to do a trial run with a piece of scrap wood to make sure you have set up properly.

2. To plane the edge molding, first run the 1/2-inch-diameter bead around the edge of the slab (see 7-13 and 7-14 left). Then use a 3/4-inch-wide cutter to clear the wood to the side of the half-round bead so that the bead stands in relief by its radius of 1/4 inch (see 7-14 right).

3. When you have achieved the edge molding profile, use the bench and block planes to shape the slopes in much the same way as you did with the base. If all is well, when the molding is seen in cross section it should read, from bottom to top, first a 1/2-inch-wide bead, then a 1/4-inch-wide flat step,

and finally a slope that angles back to a depth of about 11/2 inches (see 7-15). Aim for clean, straight miters at the corners of the slope.

Assembly and Painting

1. Once you have assembled all the component parts—the box with the base slab fitted and the lid rim with the lid slab glued and nailed in place (see 7-16)—fill all the holes and seams, especially the groove holes, then use fine-grade sandpaper to rub all the surfaces down to a good finish. Finally, fit the hinges (see 7-17), clasp, and handles (see Woodshop Techniques section).

2. Unscrew all the fittings, move the box to a dustfree area that you have set aside for painting, and give the box a couple of all-over coats of matte black paint. When the paint is dry, refit the hardware. If you are wondering why you are going to all the trouble of fitting and then removing the hardware before painting, it is so that you can fit the hinges and locks without doing damage to the paint. Be warned—if you try to shortcut this procedure and cut and fit after painting, you likely will damage the finish.

3. Draw the frame and your chosen letters up to size (see 7-3 and 7-4), make a tracing, and press-transfer the traced lines through to the lid. Make sure that the imagery is well centered and aligned.

4. Use a fine-point brush to block in the imagery with the gold paint (see 7-18). When the paint is completely dry, give the whole box a couple of coats of spar varnish.

TIPS

• If there is a lot of friction when using the combination plane, rub a candle on the side of the fence and the sole of the plane. The heat caused by the friction will melt the wax and burnish the tool, resulting in beautiful sliding action.

• Although using the molding plane is relatively easy, there are some rules of thumb beginners should follow to avoid problems: Use dry wood that is smooth grained and knot free. Make sure that the cutter blade is clean, well honed, and set for a fine cut, and that the fence is well set, clean, and burnished with candle wax. Don't press down too hard when you are making a cut.

• If you don't have a holdfast, now is the time to get one. It is wonderfully easy to use—all you do is locate the foot on the workpiece and tighten up the screw, and the workpiece is completely locked in place.

VARIATIONS

• If you want to make a box that is a bit stronger, then you could use 2-inch-thick oak throughout, with dovetail joints, and line the finished box with steel plate. You might also modify the size of the box so that it can be hidden away in a specific nook somewhere in your house.

• If you like the lettering but want to go for a swifter, easier technique, varnish the matte black ground and then try painting on top of the dry varnish. You will find that the smoother surface will result in more fluid forms. You will, of course, have to revarnish to protect the letters.

Massachusetts Knife Rack and Box

A wall box used for holding long-bladed kitchen knives, with a tray and carved pegs. Shaped with a scroll saw and knife; worked with a molding plane; butt-jointed, dovetailed, and nailed; oiled and waxed.

Early American kitchens tended to be serious workrooms where the no-nonsense business of turning basic food items into tasty dishes was conducted. There was always need for a good number of long-bladed knives—knives for butchering and boning, knives for carving, bread knives, and all manner of curved, pointed, and toothed knives for other purposes.

This knife rack and box is a clever and practical way of storing kitchen knives; the handles are on view, but the sharp blades stick down through the slots and disappear into a deep box so that they are safely out of harm's way.

DESIGN, STRUCTURE, AND TECHNIQUE

The box stands about 17½ inches high and is 10 inches wide across the span of the back board, with the base slab measuring 11¾ by 6 inches (see 8-1). Note the primary features: the molded profile around the slotted knife board and the base slab, the fancy scroll-cut head board, the basic dovetail joints for the tray, and the use throughout of nails and pegs rather than glue.

This last point is especially important, as it captures the spirit of the old-time woodworkers. The way the structure has been put together so that all the open joints, nails, and wooden pegs are on view gives the piece its naive charm.

WOOD AND MATERIALS

This project is best made in a traditional light-colored native wood, a hardwood with a vigorous grain character. We used ash for all the forward-facing boards, oak for the two molded boards, and scrap pieces of ash and oak for all the bits and pieces in between. All dimensions are slightly oversize to allow for a small amount of cutting waste.

For this project you need the following:

A 3/8-inch-thick piece of ash at 70 inches long and 5 inches wide for the two fancy back boards, the two front boards, and the front of the tray.

- A 3/4-inch-thick piece of oak at 12 by 6 inches for the base.
- A 3/4-inch-thick piece of oak at 12 by 3 inches for the slotted strip.
- A 1/4-inch-thick piece of oak at 12 by 4 inches for the sides of the tray.
- A selection of strips and scrap pieces for the inside partitions of the rack.
- Linseed oil.
- Pure beeswax polish.
- Nails.
- PVA glue.

Fig. 8-1. Working drawing, top left and right, at a grid scale of 1 square to 1 inch. Top middle, naive dovetail joint, at a grid scale of 4 squares to 1 inch. Bottom left, detail of knife slots, at a grid scale of 2 squares to 1 inch. Bottom right, detail of cross-section through the base board, at a grid scale of 4 squares to 1 inch.

Fig. 8-2. Cutting guide, at a grid scale of 1 square to 1 inch.

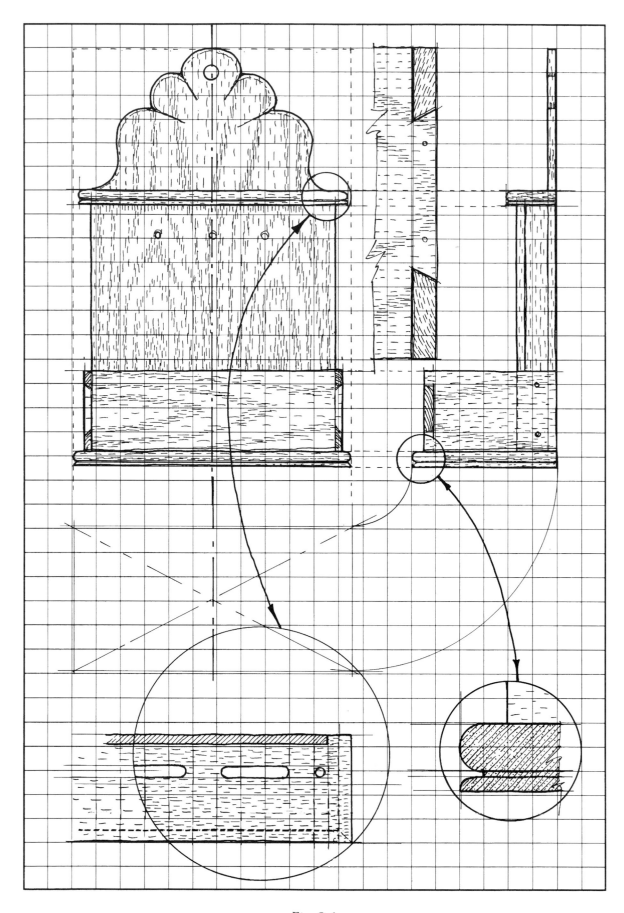

Fig. 8-1

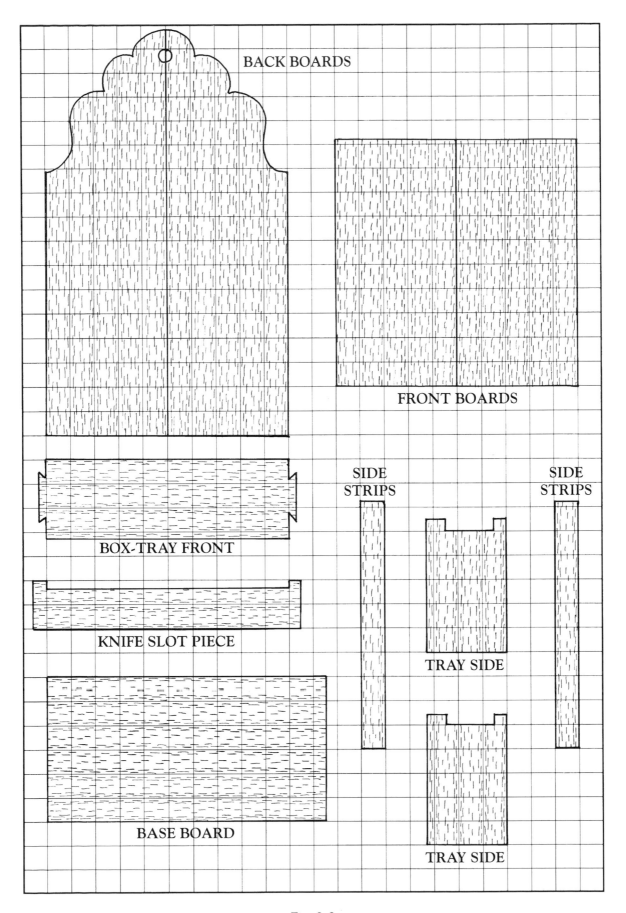

BACK BOARDS

FRONT BOARDS

BOX-TRAY FRONT

SIDE STRIPS

SIDE STRIPS

TRAY SIDE

KNIFE SLOT PIECE

BASE BOARD

TRAY SIDE

Fig. 8-2

Fig. 8-3. *Chisel off the far corners before planing the end grain on the shooting board.*

Fig. 8-5. *Arrange the partition strips so that the best faces are on view at the side edges.*

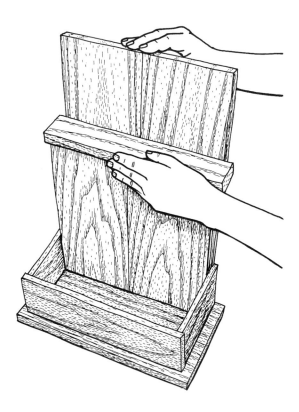

Fig. 8-4. *Arrange the boards for the best grain effect and check them for overall size.*

SUGGESTED TOOLS AND SUPPLIES

- A band saw.
- A scroll saw.
- A tenon saw.
- A pencil, ruler, and pair of dividers.
- An adjustable angle square.
- A shooting board and bench hook.
- A bench plane.
- A small block plane.
- A combination plane with a 1/2-inch-diameter bead blade (we use an old Stanley 45).
- A bench drill with 1/4-, 3/8-, and 3/4-inch Forstner bits.
- A set of chisels.
- A sheet of graph paper.
- A sheet of tracing paper.
- A joiner's hammer.
- A punch.
- All the usual workshop tools and materials, such as sandpaper and scissors.

CONSTRUCTION

Marking Out and Preparation

1. First study the project picture (see color section) and the working drawings (see 8-1

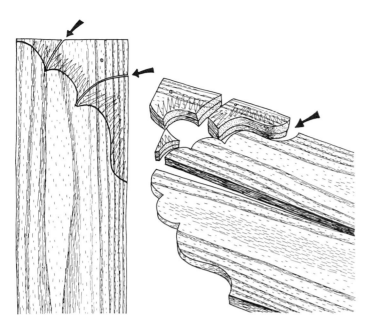

Fig. 8-6. Left, *use the band saw to cut directly into the valleys.* Right, *use the scroll saw to cut out the fancy profile. Work in the direction of the arrow.*

Fig. 8-7. *Use the square and pencil to draw guidelines, then nail the whole works together.*

and 8-2), choose your wood, sharpen your tools, and get your working area ready. Then take the prepared 5-inch-wide board of ash, mark it out, and saw it down so that you have five lengths—two at 16¾ inches for the back boards, two at 10¼ inches for the front boards, and one at 10½ inches for the front of the tray. Cut all of these boards about 1/16 inch oversize and then plane off the ends on the shooting board so that the board ends will be clean-cut and true.

2. Once the pieces are cut to size, lay them down on the shooting board and use the bench and block planes to true up the sawn ends (see 8-3).

3. When you have prepared all the primary boards that go to make up the design, test-fit them to see how the boards relate one to another (see 8-4). Arrange the boards for the best grain effect, and label edges and faces with pencil so that you know what goes where and how.

4. Cut the five 1-by-¾-inch partition strips to size. Three should be 10¼ inches long; the other two can be the same length

Fig. 8-8. *Place the wood in the vise so that the cut will be vertical.*

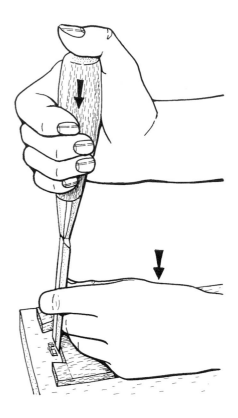

Fig. 8-9. Having used the scroll saw to remove the bulk of the waste, tidy up with the chisel. Work with a two-handed action so that the tool is safely controlled.

Fig. 8-10. Use a sash clamp to hold the waste wood firmly against the side of the workpiece to prevent the wood from splitting when the plane runs off the edge.

Fig. 8-11. Drill out the ends of each knife slot, then use the scroll saw to complete the cut. First pass the blade end through one drilled hole, refit the blade and adjust the tension, and then feed the wood so that the line of cut is slightly to the waste side of the drawn line.

or a bit shorter. Test-fit and select the best two strips for the edges that are on view (see 8-5).

Building the Knife Rack and Tray

1. Draw the fancy headboard profile up to full size, make a tracing of one half of the design, and then pencil press-transfer the imagery through to the best face of one of the two back boards.

2. Carefully shade in the area of waste that needs to be cut away, put the two boards together with the best faces on the outside, and nail them together, making sure the nails are in the waste area.

3. Cut the profile out with the band saw and scroll saw, first using the band saw to cut directly into the valleys (see 8-6 left), and then the scroll saw to cut out the curves. The initial cuts will enable you to change the direction of the scroll saw cut without the worry of breaking the blade. Once you have achieved a smooth cut, open the two boards out and see how they look (see 8-6 right).

Fig. 8-12. Ensure that the shoulders on the slot strip are an easy fit to allow for subsequent expansion and contraction of the wood.

Fig. 8-13. Hold the knife at a low angle and draw it toward your thumb. Aim to remove long slivers of wood.

4. Test-fit the two back boards, two front boards, and five filler pieces to make sure they all fit together properly. Then nail the whole structure together with 3/4-inch-long brass nails (see 8-7). First butt the two front boards together and nail them on the middle strip. Next nail the side strips and the two short strips in place. Then flip the whole arrangement over and nail on the two back boards. If you have done it right, the whole arrangement should stand true and square, with the boards being a tight fit at the center.

5. Now make the tray. First plane the boards to width, then use the shooting board and the block plane to trim the ends to size. Use the square and knife to mark out the shape of the flat dovetail.

6. Use a fine-toothed saw to cut the large dovetail (see 8-8). Then use the marking knife and the actual dovetail to transfer the shape through to the ends of the side boards. Finally, use the scroll saw to clear most of the waste, and then use the chisel to trim the key to size (see 8-9).

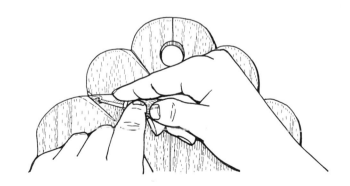

Fig. 8-14. Top left, *draw guidelines, then use a sharp knife to sink a straight-down cut along the drawn line. Decrease the depth of cut as the blade exits.* Top middle, *make a second cut at an angle to the first, again decreasing the pressure on exit.* Top right, *make a third cut to complete the notch.* Bottom, *control and steady the cuts with a two-handed grasp—one hand pulling and the other being ready to brake.*

Fig. 8-15. *Leave the dowel ends out and round over the edges.*

Making the Moldings and Cutting the Knife Slots

1. Make sure your molding plane is in good condition. Then fit the 1/2-inch-diameter half-round beading blade and adjust both the fence and the depth stop so that you can run the beading to one edge of the 3/4-inch-thick workpiece.

2. Set the 3/4-inch-thick 111/2-by-6-inch slab of oak in the bench vise with the long side uppermost, butt the plane fence firmly against what will be the top or best face of the wood, and then make a series of light cuts to shape the profile.

3. When you have cut the front-of-base profile, reposition the wood so that one end-grain edge is uppermost, clamp a waste piece in front of the wood to prevent end-grain split-off (see 8-10), and then work the molding (see 8-1 bottom right). Repeat these procedures for all the molded edges.

4. Once the moldings have been cleanly cut on the three visible edges of both the base and the knife-slot strip, take the knife-slot strip and use a pencil, ruler, square, and knife to mark out the positions of the cut-back shoulder line and the slots. If you are going to use this project in your kitchen for your own knives, adjust the size of the slots accordingly.

5. Cut the slots, first drilling out each end of the slot with the 1/4-inch-diameter Forstner bit, and then linking pairs of holes with scroll saw cuts. It's a little bit finger-twisting, because you have to keep unhitching the scroll saw blade and passing one end through the hole (see 8-11), but you shouldn't have any problems if you work at a slow, easy pace.

Assembly and Finishing

1. Before you do anything else, go to the drill press and make all the holes. You need a 3/4-inch-diameter hole in the center of the fancy head board, three 3/8-inch-diameter holes set in a line for the pegs, and various peg-fixing holes (see 8-1).

2. Set the knife-slot piece on top of the hollow board, adjust the shoulders for the best fit, and secure it in place with a couple of brass nails (see 8-12).

3. Carve and whittle three good-size pegs from a scrap of oak and tap them in place. Aim for a bold shape and a tight push-fit (see 8-13). Cut them to fit your own needs. For example, I'm going to use mine for various household keys, but you might want larger pegs for, say, your pastry cutters.

4. With the pegs fitted, mark out the position of the board on the base slab, nail a couple of 3/4-inch-wide bits of scrap on the base, slide the hollow knife board in place on the blocks, and secure it with a handful of brass nails.

5. Use the knife to trim and embellish the head board (see 8-14).

6. Nail and dowel the dovetailed tray in place on the base slab (see 8-15), and rub the whole workpiece down to a smooth finish.

7. Lay on a thin coat of linseed oil, let it dry, and burnish the whole works with beeswax polish.

TIPS

• If you don't have access to a band saw and scroll saw, you could use a gents hand saw for the straight cuts, and a hand coping or small bow saw for the curves.

• If you just acquired your molding plane, it's a good idea to spend some time practicing with it on scrap wood before attempting this project. When you are experimenting with the various cuts, pay particular attention to the position of the sledge runners and the setting of the spur cutter.

• We always use Forstner drill bits. Even though they are about twice the price of twist bits or spade bits, they cut clean, beautiful holes and last just about forever.

• If you don't have the use of a molding plane, you could use a knife or bench plane to cut a round-nosed edge.

VARIATIONS

• Although we like to use brass nails, which over time stain the wood and add character, you could make a more sophisticated project and use glue and flush dowels.

• If your knives have longer blades or fatter handles, you will need to modify the dimensions of the rack accordingly.

Pencil Box

Traditionally a box used by schoolchildren for holding their pens and pencils. Shaped with a scroll saw; worked with a spokeshave, plane, and drill; decorated with a gouge; oiled and waxed.

Not so long ago, between about 1880 and 1940, just about every schoolchild had a little wooden box in his or her school desk for holding pens and pencils. These boxes were about 10 to 12 inches long and 2 to 3 inches wide. The lid slid back to reveal a tray for holding three or four pencils. When this top layer was pivoted to one side, there was a second tray for pens and nibs. Some boxes had three or four layers, with additional compartments for erasers and pencil sharpeners.

I still have my own box, which was my grandfather's. It has a picture on the lid entitled "General Gordon—Omdorman," which dates it to about 1898. The joy of these boxes lies in their "secret" trays—perfect for storing chewing gum, dead beetles, or other treasures.

DESIGN, STRUCTURE, AND TECHNIQUE

The box is $9^{1}/2$ inches long, $2^{3}/8$ inches wide, and $1^{1}/4$ inches deep (see 9-1). Note the way it is laminated up from three layers. The center area of the middle layers is cut out, and the top layer is fretted so that the lid is held in place by a mitered lip. The ends of the box are decorated with gouged scallops.

Of all the projects in the book, this box is at the same time one of the most sophisticated and one of the easiest—a large drill bit and a scroll saw, and you are on your way!

WOOD AND MATERIALS

The wood needs to be hard in texture, smooth grained, knotfree, and split resistant, so this project is best made from a traditional hardwood like cherry, plum, or even maple. We have chosen cherry. The wood needs to be oversize so that the box can be cut back to a good finish.

For this project you need the following:
• Two $^{3}/8$-inch-thick pieces of cherry at 12 inches long and $2^{1}/2$ inches wide for the lid and the base boards.
• A $3/4$-inch-thick piece of cherry at 12 inches long and $2^{1}/2$ inches wide for the central section.
• Danish oil.
• Pure beeswax polish.

SUGGESTED TOOLS AND SUPPLIES
• A scroll saw.
• A tenon saw.
• A pencil, ruler, and compass.
• An adjustable angle square.
• A shooting board with bench hook.
• A bench plane or a portable surface planer.
• A small block plane.
• A bench drill with a $1^{5}/8$-inch-diameter Forstner bit.
• A small scoop gouge bout $^{3}/16$ inch wide.
• A spokeshave.

Fig. 9-1. Working drawing, top, at a grid scale of 2 squares to 1 inch and bottom, 4 grid squares to 1 inch. Note how the success of the project has to do primarily with the sandwiching procedure.

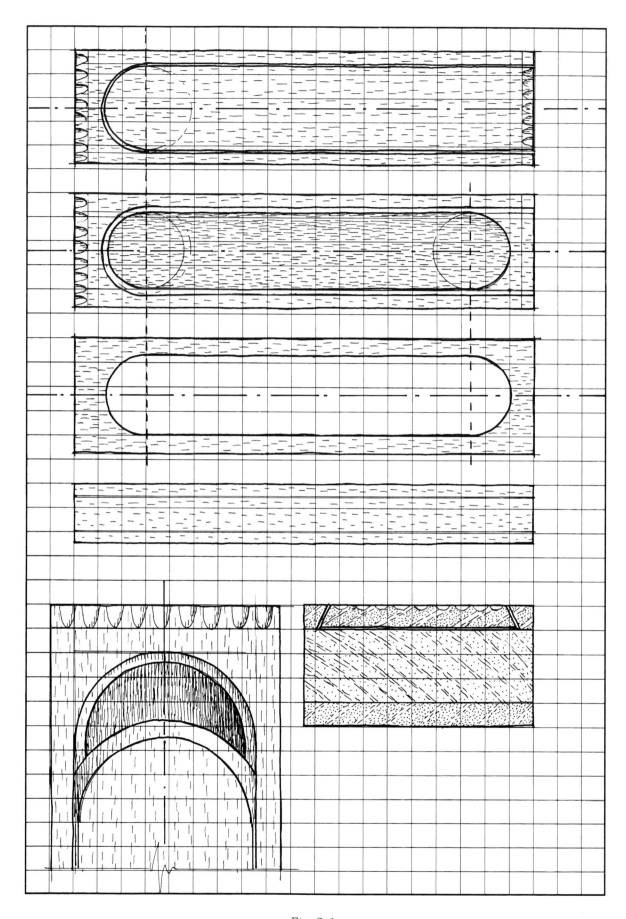

Fig. 9-1

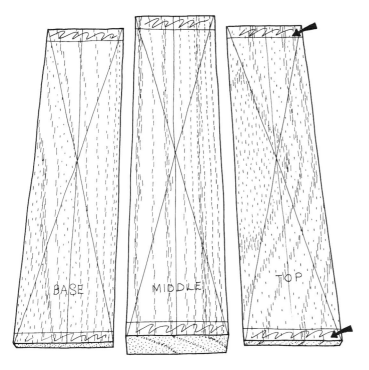

Fig. 9-2. Establish the centerlines, square off the centers, and draw in as many guidelines as you think necessary. Label the parts and shade in areas of waste.

Fig. 9-3. It is important that the two holes be crisply and cleanly cut, so it's best to use a Forstner bit.

- A sheet of graph paper.
- A sheet of tracing paper.
- All the usual workshop tools and materials, such as sandpaper, dividers, and scissors.

CONSTRUCTION

Marking Out and Preparation

1. First study the working drawings (see 9-1) and draw the design up to full size. Take your chosen three pieces of wood and check them over to make sure that they are free from splits, then use a pencil to label the three boards "base," "middle," and "top."

2. Set all three boards out with centerlines that run along the length of the grain, use a square to establish the ends, and shade in the waste (see 9-2). Aim for a total box length of 9$\frac{1}{2}$ to 10 inches.

3. Use the pencil, ruler, compass, and square to mark the middle board with all the guidelines necessary to make the cutout (see 9-1). Establish center points at each end so that the total length of the cavity finishes up at no less than 8$\frac{3}{8}$ inches.

Fig. 9-4. If you feel the saw blade running wildly off course as mine did, be sure the faulty sawn line runs to the waste side of the drawn line.

Fig. 9-5. Use a spokeshave to clean up the sawn faces of the cavity.

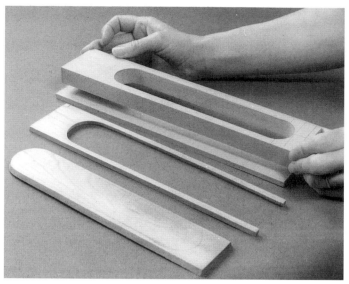

Fig. 9-7. Sand all the surfaces to a good finish. Make sure that the mating faces are level.

Fig. 9-6. Fret out the lid so that the sawn edge angles down and out from the best face of the lid.

Cutting the Cavity

1. Fix the centerpoints for the two holes, then move to the drill press and bore out the two holes.

2. Set a piece of scrap wood under the workpiece to minimize damage when the drill bit exits, securely clamp the whole arrangement to the drill press worktable, and do your best to sink two clean-cut holes (see 9-3).

3. Now use the scroll saw to cut away the waste from between the holes. It's fairly easy: Unhitch the saw blade, pass it through one or the other of the holes, rehitch and retension the blade, and then start sawing. Be sure to cut on the waste side of the drawn line in case your cut is a bit wobbly like mine was (see 9-4). Be sure to start with a new blade. If you plan to spend your holiday building boxes, when the shops may be closed, have a pack of spare blades on hand.

4. Secure the workpiece on its side edge and use the spokeshave or a tube rasp to clean up the sawn faces of the cavity. Work from the ends to the center (see 9-5).

Making the Lid

1. Before you do anything else, carefully examine the working drawings and note how

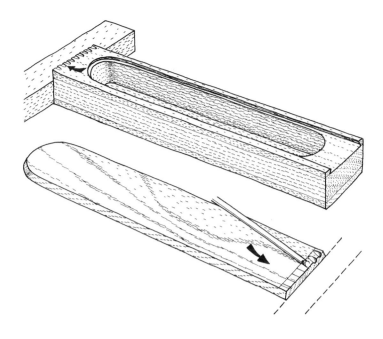

Fig. 9-8. *Use a razor-sharp small U-section gouge to cut the decorative notches.*

the lid is contained and held by being slightly wider than the cavity and mitered at the edges (see 9-1 bottom).

2. Use the pencil, ruler, square, and compass to lay out the lid shape on the best face of the top board. Tilt and adjust your scroll saw table over at an angle—mine tilts down to the left (see 9-6)—and fret out the lid.

3. Keeping in mind that the lid edge miter needs to undercut the frame, slowly run the line of cut along the drawn line. This procedure is slightly complicated, as the workpiece continually tries to slide down the slope, and the design is such that you can't afford to wander off course. Be sure to start out with a new fine-toothed blade, make sure it is well tensioned, and don't force the rate of cut.

Assembly

1. Once you have completed the four component parts that go to make the project—the bottom, middle section, top frame, and lid (see 9-7)—test-fit to see how everything comes together. When you are sure that all the pieces fit together properly, use a soft-lead pencil to label the faces that are to be glued together so that you'll be able to see at a glance how the box fits together.

2. Take the middle section, and use a scrap of fine-grade sandpaper to rub the top rim edge of the cavity down to a smooth, round-edged finish. Sand all the surfaces of all four pieces, making sure they are smooth and clean. Pay particular attention to the edges of the lid and its frame.

3. Smear a small amount of glue on mating faces, put the sandwich together, and clamp up. Carefully wipe off any excess glue from the cavity and the inside edge of the lid frame. Don't worry about the glue that oozes out from the sides of the sandwich, but do make sure that the sides of the lid frame are correctly aligned.

4. Wait for the glue to set, then trim the ends of the box block to size and use the block plane to skim off all the outside faces.

5. Use the square to draw in guidelines for the decorative notches. Then butt the workpiece firmly against the bench stop and use the gouge to make the cuts. Aim for swift, clean cuts that run off the ends to a depth of about 1/16 inch (see 9-8).

6. Give the whole works a couple of thin coats of Danish oil, let it dry, and then use the beeswax to burnish all the surfaces to a dull sheen finish.

TIPS

• If you are a beginner to the fretsaw or any other power tool, it's always a good idea to spend time exploring its potential. Be certain to read the manufacturer's instruction manual before you switch on the power.

• If you do not have the use of a scroll saw, you could always use a hand coping saw or a fretsaw.

• If the lid is a bit on the loose side, give the mitered edges of the lid and frame, as well as the underside face of the lid, a couple of extra coats of Danish oil.

VARIATIONS

• If you are a beginner with a minimal took kit, you could build the whole box up from 1/4-inch-thick layers. You could create a very fancy box by laminating alternate light and dark woods.

Cottage Writing Box

A table box traditionally used for holding all the paraphernalia related to letter writing—
paper, stamps, sticky labels, ink, pen holders, and steel nibs.
Cut on a band saw; worked with a plane and chisel; butt-jointed; glued and nailed;
varnished, combed, beeswaxed, and burnished.

By the late nineteenth century, just about every American family could read and write at least a little. With this increased literacy, plus improved transport, most families wanted at some time or other to write letters. Thus it became fashionable to have a writing box. Those who could afford it had fancy boxes perhaps made of mahogany and decorated with fruitwood inlays; those with less money made do with pine boxes that were skillfully made up to look like expensive wood. Those who were clever with their hands might look in a catalog and make their own copies from some thin crate wood.

Our box draws its inspiration from such an original; it is made from thin pine salvaged from an old fruit box, with nailed butt joints and a combed finish.

DESIGN, STRUCTURE, AND TECHNIQUE

The box measures about 5¼ inches high, 14¼ inches wide across the span of the front key board, and 8¾ inches from front to back when closed, with the base measuring 14¼ by 8¾ inches (see 10-3). When the whole box is opened, it covers an area of 14¼ by 17½ inches and looks very much like a small writing desk. It is very simply fitted out with a raised shelf at the top end for ink pots, stamps, clips, and pens. The pen tray is fitted on tip-up runners to create a secret compartment. The naive finish is easily and swiftly achieved with varnish and a steel comb.

WOOD AND MATERIALS

For authenticity, we wanted to make this project as a poor settler might have, so we used salvaged wood throughout. We used the wood from an old pine fruit box for the body of the box, 3/16 inch and ½ inch thick; a couple of sheets of 1/8-inch-thick plywood for the writing surfaces; various odds and ends of wood; and a couple of rather bruised brass hinges.

For this project you need the following:

- A quantity of ½-inch-thick wood for the front, back, and sides of the box.
- A quantity of 3/16-inch-thick wood for the lid, base, and dividing strips.
- A couple of 1/8-inch-thick sheets of plywood for the inside-box writing surface.
- Various scrap pieces of wood.
- A can of tinted brown-red varnish.
- Beeswax polish.
- Nails.
- PVA glue.

Fig. 10-1. Working drawing, at a grid scale of 1 square to 1 inch. Note the naive hammer-and-nails structure.

Fig. 10-2. Cutting guide, at a grid scale of 1 square to 1 inch. The diagram offers a suggestion on how to size the inside compartments of the box, but you might want to change measurements to suit your needs.

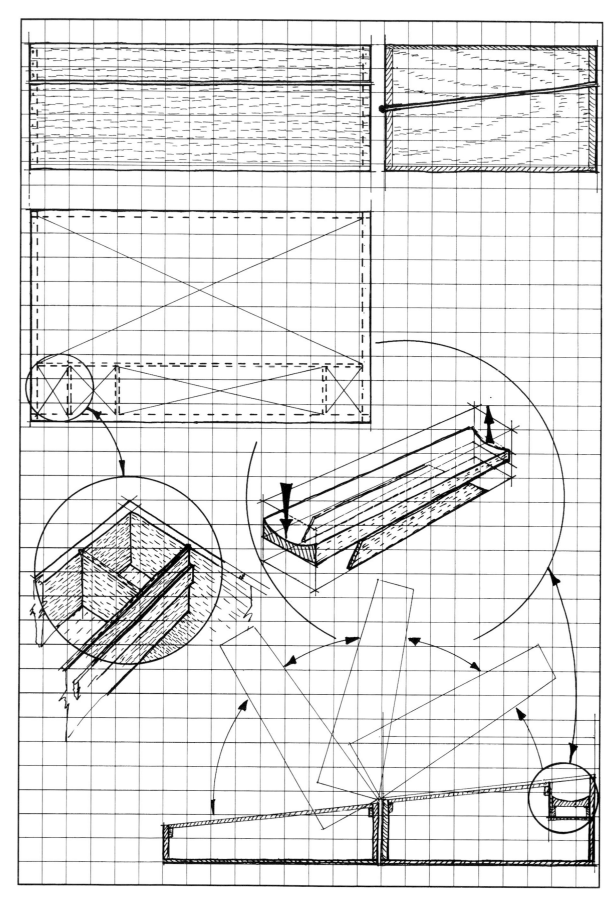

Fig. 10-1

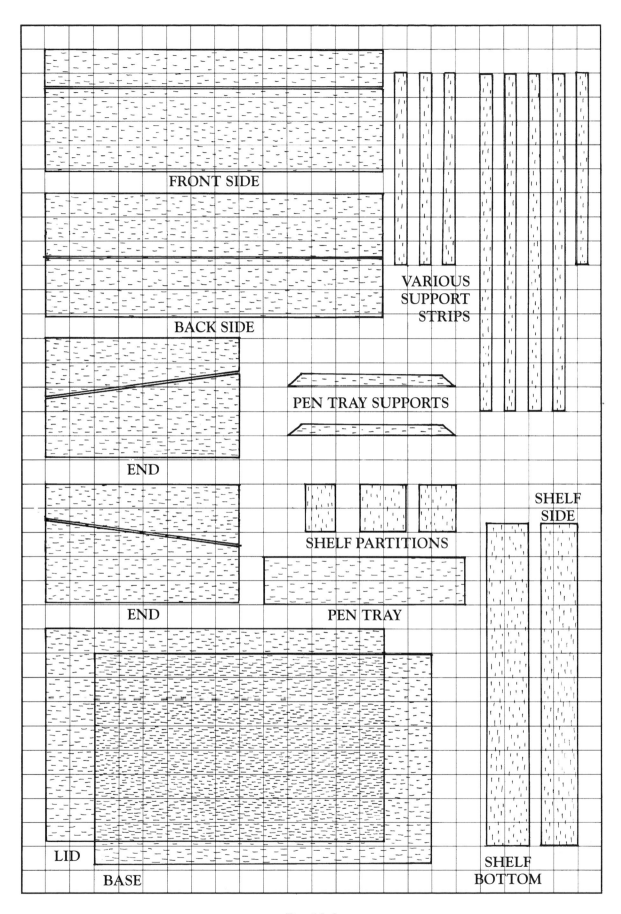

FRONT SIDE

BACK SIDE

END

END

LID

BASE

VARIOUS
SUPPORT
STRIPS

PEN TRAY SUPPORTS

SHELF PARTITIONS

PEN TRAY

SHELF
SIDE

SHELF
BOTTOM

Fig. 10-2

Fig. 10-3. The primary component parts that go to make the box front and sides, and the thin strips that are needed to support the writing surface.

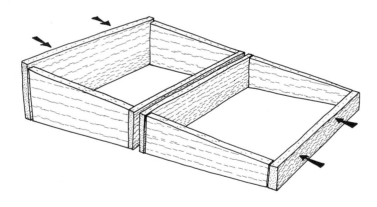

Fig. 10-4. Place and push the sides together to see how they fit.

Fig. 10-5. Cut the lid and base boards so that they are generously oversize.

SUGGESTED TOOLS AND SUPPLIES
- A workbench with a vise and holdfast.
- A band saw.
- A selection of handsaws.
- A pencil, ruler, and compass.
- An adjustable angle square.
- A good sharp knife for marking out.
- A shooting board or shooting bench hook.
- A bench plane.
- A small block plane.
- A set of chisels.
- A shallow-sweep straight gouge.
- A V-section gouge.
- A selection of different length panel nails.
- A small hammer.
- A sheet of graph paper.
- A sheet of tracing paper.
- A variety of clamps.
- All the usual workshop tools and materials, such as sandpaper, dividers, and scissors.

CONSTRUCTION
Preparing the Wood and Box Assembly

1. First study the project photographs (see color section) and the working drawings (see 10-1), and decide on the size of your box. Then take your salvaged crate wood and

Fig. 10-6. Punch the nails down below the surface.

Fig. 10-7. Place the two halves together and check for fit and squareness.

check it over for potential problems. Remove all nails, staples, and labels. So that you don't ruin your plane blade on a piece of buried metal, use an electrician's metal detector to search out hidden nails. Plug any old nail holes with glue-dipped splinters.

2. Plane the surfaces down to a good finish, and use the pencil, ruler, square, and knife to mark out all the lines that go to make up the design. In addition to the two pieces of plywood that will form the writing surface, the top and bottom of the box, and the short partition strips, you will have fourteen pieces: four 1/2-inch-thick strips for the front and back boards, four 1/2-inch-thick angled strips for the box ends, two 3/16-inch-thick strips for the main partition, and four narrow 3/16-inch-thick strips for the writing surface supports (see 10-3).

3. Use the shooting board and the block plane to skim the end-grain edges down to a smooth finish, and then test-fit the pieces. Ask a friend to help hold the pieces together while you check with the square to make sure all components are true and the correct length (see 10-4).

4. Try out the bottom and top boards for size (see 10-5) and make sure everything has been cut properly.

Fig. 10-8. Steady the V-section tool with one hand and push with the other. Make several passes until you have enough depth.

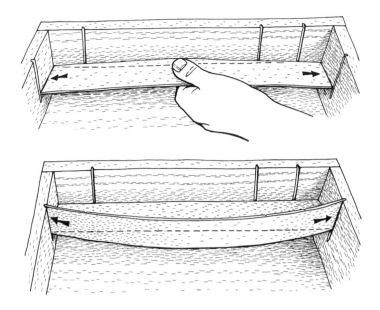

Fig. 10-11. Glue and clamp.

Fig. 10-9. Top, *spring in the strip that makes the shelf base*. Bottom, *slide and spring the wall in place. To get a tight fit, trim back the ends of the strip and make the V-grooves deeper.*

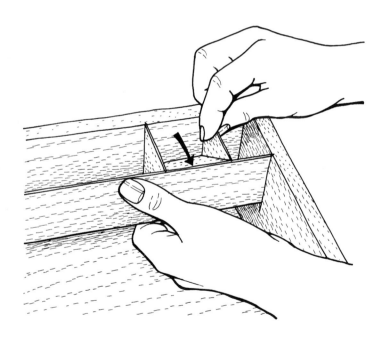

Fig. 10-10. Fit and slide the small subdivisions in place. Note the little surface that is set across the diagonals to make the stamp slide.

5. When you are sure that all is correct, smear a small amount of glue on the butt joints and nail the box together. The best procedure is to start with the box corners, and then secure the right angles by nailing on the top and bottom boards (see 10-6).

6. Finally, set the two box shapes one on top of the other (see 10-7), check for squareness, and use as many clamps as you think necessary to pull the whole works together.

Fitting the Compartment

1. Cut the two long dividing strips so that they are just a shade too long. Mark out the position of the various pen and ink compartments, then use the knife and the V-tool to cut V-section location grooves on the inside face of the box (see 10-8).

2. Chamfer off the ends of the strips so that they are V-pointed in section, and slide them in position in the box. The best sequence is to first spring in the strips that make the shelf base, and then slide in the wall (see 10-9), and finally fit the small subdivisions (see 10-

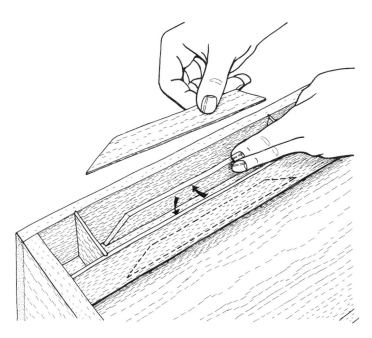

Fig. 10-12. Glue and nail the pen tray supports on each side of the long compartment. They need to be placed at center.

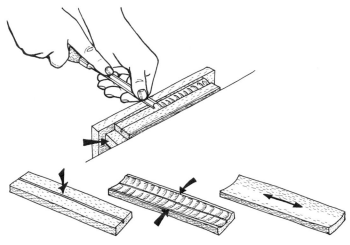

Fig. 10-13. Top, use double-sided tape to stick the pen tray to a length of waste wood, so that it is held in the vise while you work. Bottom left, saw a pilot trench to set the depth—not quite as deep as the required scoop. Bottom middle, draw guidelines for the side margins, and then use a shallow-sweep straight gouge to systematically clear the waste. Bottom right, scrape and sand the pen tray to a smooth finish.

10). Glue a small scrap inside one of the compartments to make the stamp slide.

3.   When you are pleased with the arrangement, smear a small amount of glue on all the edges and joints, and clamp the whole shelf assembly (see 10-11).

Making and Fitting the Pen Tray
1.   When the glue has set, cut a couple of 1/4-by-1-inch strips that are about 1 inch shorter than the pen tray compartment, angle off the ends at about 45 degrees, and glue and nail them in place (see 10-12).

2.   Cut a 1/2-inch-thick, 17/8-inch-wide strip to fit the long compartment so that it's a loose easy fit, and then use a saw and gouge, plane, or router to carve it to a shallow concave section (see 10-13).

3.   With the tray crisply shaped in cross section, trim it to fit the compartment. You should be able to press down on one end of the pen tray so that it seesaws up to reveal the little secret cavity (see 10-14).

Fitting the Writing Surface Boards and Finishing
1.   Fit the hinges and cut the recess in readiness for the brass lock (see Woodshop

Fig. 10-14. Press down on one end of the tray to reveal the secret compartment.

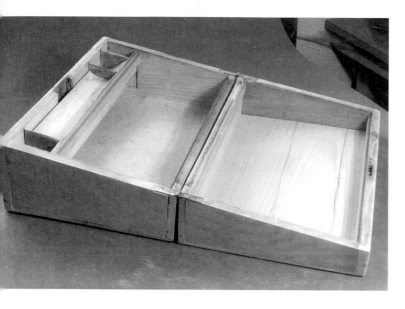

Fig. 10-15. *Glue writing surface support strips on the inside front and back.*

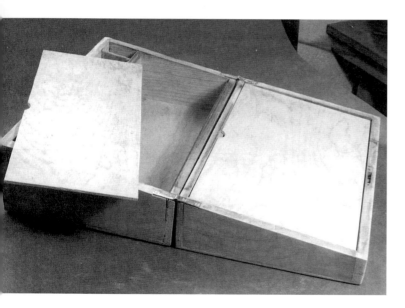

Fig. 10-16. *Cut the writing surfaces to fit. Note the little finger holes for lifting the boards.*

Techniques section). Then glue and nail the thin ledge strips in place so that the writing surface finishes up flush with the rim (see 10-15). Cut the plywood boards to size (see 10-16).

2. Sand all the surfaces down to a smooth finish, then wipe away the dust and move to a clean, dustfree area for painting.

3. Give the whole inside of the box a swift all-over coat of varnish. Take note of the drying time, from the moment you apply the varnish to the point where it is tacky and nonrunny.

4. Give the outside of the box a coat of varnish, wait until it reaches the tacky stage, then take the metal graining comb and run a series of wavy squiggles backward and forward across the width of the box. Repeat this procedure on all edges and on both sides of the writing surfaces.

5. Finally, rub the whole box down with fine-grade sandpaper, apply a generous coat of beeswax polish, and burnish all the surfaces to a rich sheen finish.

TIP

• If your writing surfaces are a bit loose, as ours are, you could give them a tight spring fit or fix them in place with hook-and-eye catches.

VARIATIONS

• If you want a fancier box, you could use plum or pencil cedar. Avoid endangered woods like mahogany. A lot of crates are made from beautiful woods. Japanese motorcycle crates are sometimes made from an attractive close-grained hardwood.

• If you want to give your project a dynamic folk art finish, refer to the reading list at the end of the book.

• Traditionally, professional box makers built just one box and then cut it through to make the lid and the base. If you want to make your project in this manner, be sure to divide the hinge side of the box into two equal halves.

• If you wish, you can cover the writing surfaces with thin leather or veneer. Be sure to allow for the additional thickness when you fit the ledge strips.

Six-Board Chest

A six-board chest made from salvaged pine floorboards.
Shaped with a knife, spokeshave, plane, and gouge; butt-jointed; glued and nailed;
painted and stippled.

Of all the boxes found in ordinary American homes—farmhouses, home-steads, and cottages—the six-board chest is the oldest and most common. Some-times made of hardwoods like oak, elm, and maple, but usually made of pine, these chests are often referred to as "poor man's furniture." This is doubtless because chests of this type can very easily be built straight from the tree using nothing more than a saw, hammer, and gouge. It is even possible to build the chest—all six sides—from the same plank width, and the whole chest can be put together without having to cut joints. In times past, if a poor man wanted to build a sturdy box that would double as a bench seat, he would almost cer-tainly have made a six-board chest.

DESIGN, STRUCTURE, AND TECHNIQUE

The chest is about 36 inches long, 16 inches wide across the width of the lid, and 19 inches in total height (see 11-1 and 11-2).

No doubt you are wondering why we have used more than six boards to make a six-board chest. Well, the ideal is to use 12-inch-wide boards, but our woodshop is full of old 6-inch-wide floorboards, and we felt that using two 6-inch planks set side by side for each 12-inch board doesn't veer too far from authenticity.

Once we were committed to using 6-inch-wide boards, we decided to change the struc-ture somewhat. The lid is built from three boards that have been glued and butt-jointed, and the sides and ends are each built from two board widths. We also have simplified

construction by cutting out the fancy foot shape before gluing the end boards together.

WOOD AND MATERIALS

For this project, we decided to use old pine floorboards. Once they have been planed on one side, they are about 7/8 inch thick.

If you decide to use old wood, be sure to remove all nails. Be warned: although we use a little metal detector to search out the nails, we still come across an occasional buried nail that makes a mess of the plane blade.

For this project you need the following:
• Six 7/8-inch-thick boards at 37 inches long and 6 inches wide for the two long sides and the base.
• Four 7/8-inch-thick boards at 18 inches long and 6 inches wide for the ends of the chest.
• Three 7/8-inch-thick boards at 38 inches long and 6 inches wide for the lid slab.
• Short lengths of wood for the cross members.
• Teak oil.
• A small tube of artists' burnt umber oil paint.

Fig. 11-1. Working drawing, top, *at a grid scale of 1 square to 2 inches and* bottom, *4 squares to 1 inch.*

Fig. 11-2. Working drawing, at a grid scale of 4 squares to 1 inch.

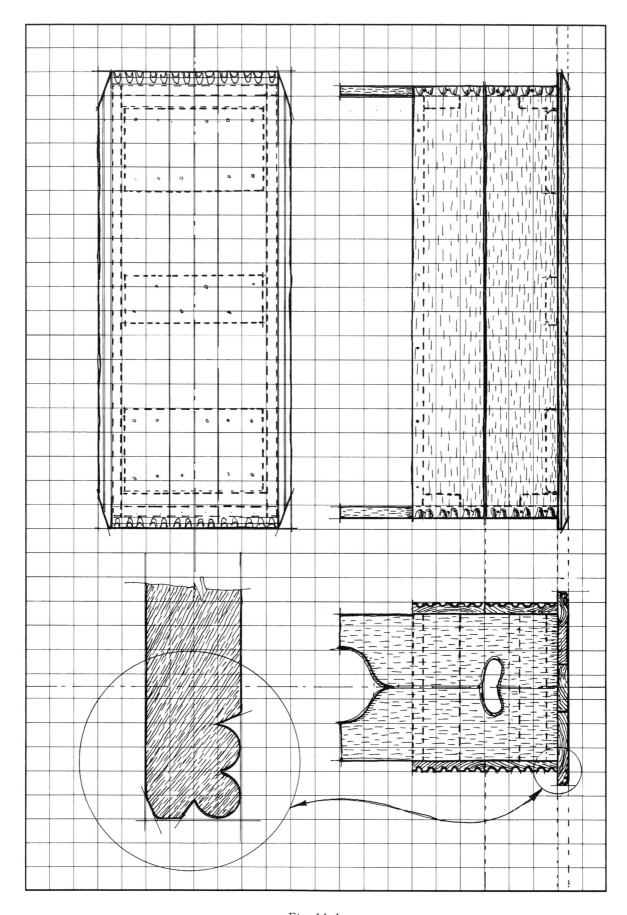

Fig. 11-1

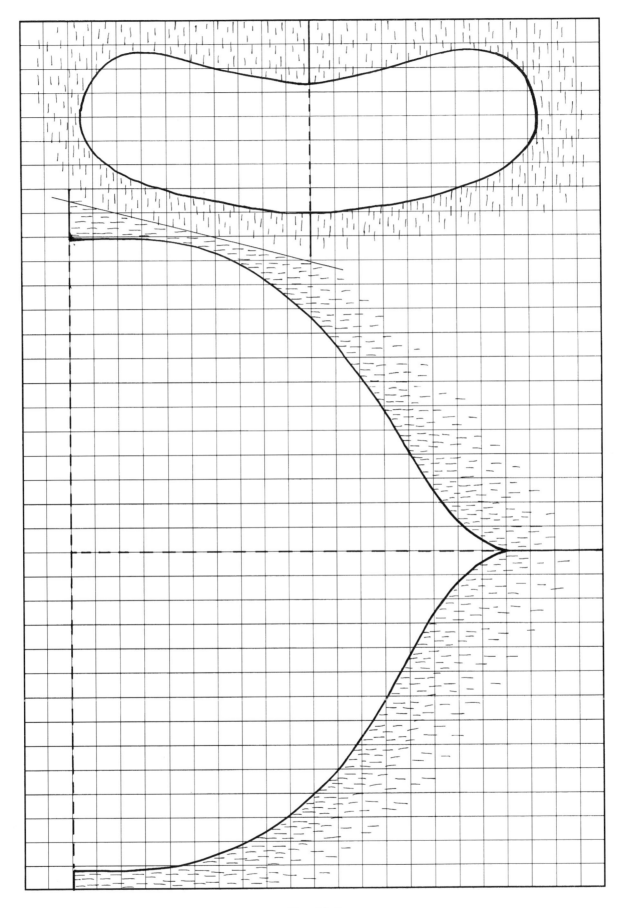

Fig. 11-2

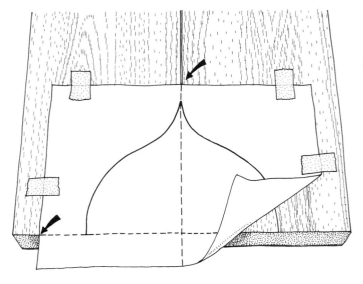

Fig. 11-3. Clamp the boards together. Then place the tracing carefully, with the center and base lines matching, and transfer the design through to the surface of the wood.

Fig. 11-5. Clamp the boards at side and center with bar clamps and two G-clamps. Set the central clamp on the opposite side of the wood to prevent the boards from springing or warping out of place.

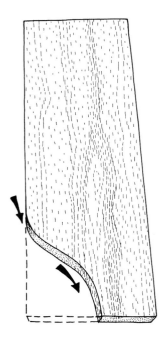

Fig. 11-4. Cut in the direction of the arrows—from high to low grain—and remove the waste wood.

- A small can of matte black oil paint.
- Nails.
- PVA glue.

SUGGESTED TOOLS AND SUPPLIES
- An electric band saw.
- A pencil, ruler, and compass.
- An adjustable angle square.
- A marking knife.
- A bench plane.
- A small block plane.
- A drill press with a 1 1/4-inch-diameter Forstner bit.
- A spokeshave—metal or wood.
- A U-section carving gouge.
- A tube surform rasp.
- A combination plane with a bead cutter (we use an old Stanley 45).
- A mallet.
- A good selection of sash clamps and G-clamps.
- A sheet of graph paper.
- A sheet of tracing paper.
- All the usual workshop tools and materials, such as sandpaper, dividers, scissors, and brushes.

Fig. 11-6. Pull the spokeshave toward your body. Aim for a crisp half-round profile.

Fig. 11-7. Punch the nail heads below the surface. Note the drawn guideline that marks the position of the bottom board.

CONSTRUCTION

Preparing the Boards

1. First study the working drawings (see 11-1 and 11-2) and gather your tools and materials. Check your wood over for problems. Wood with holes and knots is fine, but reject wood that looks split.

2. Plane all the boards on one face and both edges, and cut to length so that the ends are square. Take the 18-inch-long end boards and pair them up so that the good face is uppermost. Try to have the best square edges at center. Label the boards with pencil so that you know how they relate to each other.

Cutting and Shaping the Feet

1. Draw the fancy foot cutout to size (see 11-2 bottom), make a tracing, and then pencil press-transfer the traced lines onto the chest ends (see 11-3). Aim for a symmetrical form.

2. Cut the curves on the band saw and regroup (see 11-4).

3. When you are happy with the curves, smear glue on the mating edges and clamp up. Arrange the clamps so as to prevent the

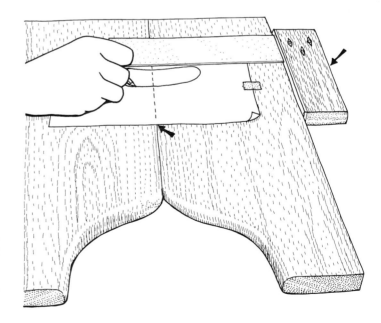

Fig. 11-8. Using a try square as a guide, mark the position of the handle hole.

Fig. 11-9. *Lap the drilled holes so as to remove the bulk of the waste. Use a piece of waste wood to prevent drill exit splinter.*

Fig. 11-11. *Punch the nail heads below the surface.*

Fig. 11-10. *Secure the two end boards side by side to make it easier to match the handle holes.*

two boards from buckling across the width (see 11-5).

4. When the glue has set, secure the board in the bench vise so that one side of the foot curve is angling toward you and is at a comfortable working angle, and then shave off the edges of the curve with the spokeshave (see 11-6). Try to achieve a half-round profile. Use a knife to reach up into the peak. Repeat the process for both sides of each foot curve. To make this step easier, you could shape the foot before gluing up. You would then be able to get the spokeshave right up into the peak.

5. After both feet are shaped, lay the chest down with the underside up, and glue and nail two 3- to 4-inch-wide strengthening pieces across the width (see 11-7). Place them so that one is flush with the top edge and the other aligned with what will be the position of the bottom of the box (see 11-1).

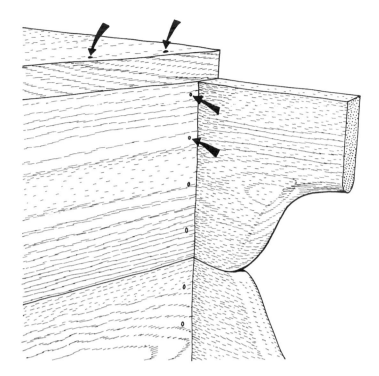

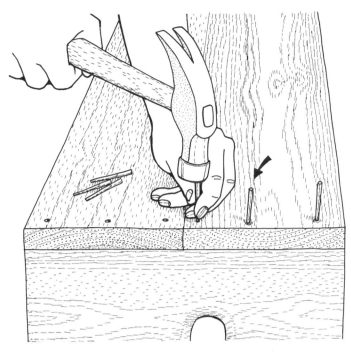

Fig. 11-12. Nail the base boards in place through the bottom edge of the side boards and up into the end board strengtheners.

Fig. 11-13. Glue and hammer the pegs into the nail holes.

Cutting and Shaping the Handle Holes

1. Turn the chest ends over so that the best face is up, and press-transfer the shape of the handle hole through to the wood (see 11-8). Use a square to make sure the holes are both well placed. Shade in the inside of the holes to be cut away.

2. Lay the workpiece on a piece of waste so that the wood at the back of the handle hole is well supported, and use the drill press and the 1 1/4-inch-diameter Forstner bit to bore out the waste. Lap the drilled holes, one over the other (see 11-9).

3. Clean up the edges of the handle holes with a knife or gouge, then secure the two boards side by side in the bench vise with the feet uppermost. Use the knife, rasp, and sandpaper to work the holes to a good-to-hold matching finish (see 11-10).

Fig. 11-14. Use the spokeshave to bring the faces to a smooth finish.

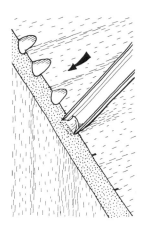

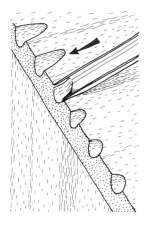

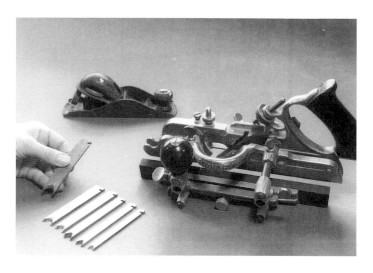

Fig. 11-17. *Select a blade from the Stanley 45 range.*

Fig. 11-15. Left, *mark in the step-off guidelines and use the gouge and mallet to chop out the decorative edge.* Right, *repeat the procedure to achieve deeper and wider cuts.*

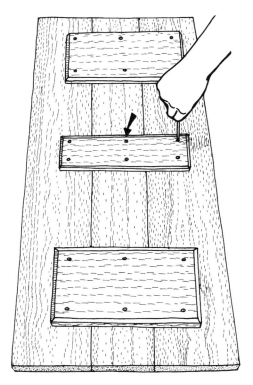

Fig. 11-16. *Drill and screw the strengthener braces onto the underside of the lid. Leave enough space for the thickness on the ends of the box.*

Assembling the Chest and Cutting the Decorative Notches

1. When you have achieved two well-matched chest ends, take the 36-inch-long side boards and nail them in place to form a box shape. The best procedure is to drive in one nail per board, then check for squareness and alignment before driving in the other nails. When you are sure that all is correct, punch the nail heads down below the surface (see 11-11).

2. Turn the chest upside down and cut and fit the base boards. Attach them at the ends with nails that run up into the end strengtheners, and run nails down through the bottom edge of the side boards and into the base boards (see 11-12).

3. When you have achieved a form that is strong and stable, make a little stack of knife-cut pegs and go over the workpiece filling in all the nail holes. The best procedure is to cut the dowels oversize, then dip them in glue and drive them home with a hammer (see 11-13). Fill in any remaining splits or holes with wood filler.

4. Wait for the glue and filler to dry, then saw the pegs off as close as you can to the sur-

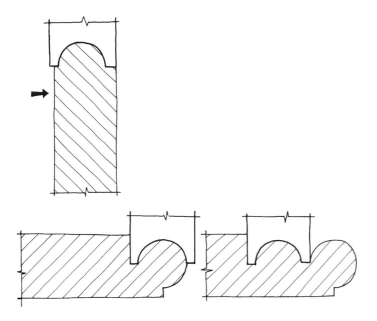

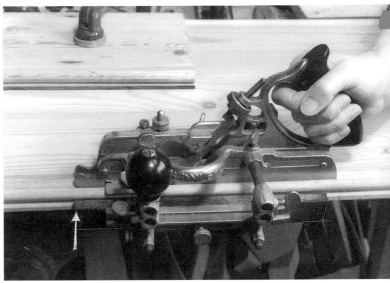

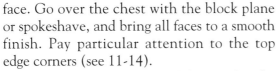

Fig. 11-18. Top, *cut a bead on the leading edge.* Left, *cut a second bead on the face of the board so as to completely round the first bead.* Right, *cut another bead alongside the first.*

Fig. 11-19. *The fence, noted by the arrow, needs to be held firmly against the workpiece. (Note that Gill has removed one hand here so that you can see what's going on.)*

face. Go over the chest with the block plane or spokeshave, and bring all faces to a smooth finish. Pay particular attention to the top edge corners (see 11-14).

5. Finally, being very careful not to hit the hidden nails, use the mallet and U-section gouge to cut the line of notches that decorate the ends of the side boards (see 11-15). Don't worry if you have to space the cuts to avoid the nails. Place the notches so that there are about six or seven per 6-inch board width.

Making the Lid

1. Prepare and plane the three lid boards. Then place them side by side with the best edges outermost. Make sure that the edges that will be worked with the molding plane are as free as possible from holes and knots. Glue the boards edge to edge.

2. When the glue has set, carefully cut the slab to length. Chamfer the edges of the brace pieces to a decorative finish. Glue and screw the braces across the width on the underside, one at each end and one in the middle (see 11-16). The cross braces should fit neatly into

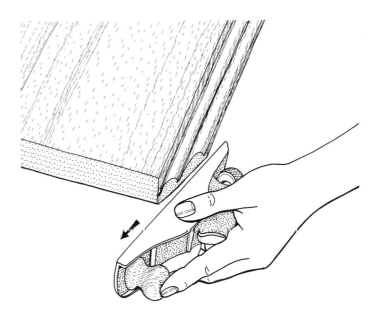

Fig. 11-20. *Use the block plane to nip off the corners of the lid.*

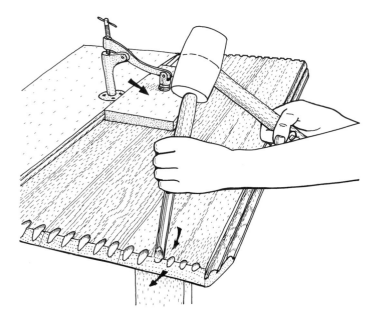

Fig. 11-21. Chamfer the end edge, then use the gouge to cut the decorative notches. Chamfer the corners.

the top of the chest. Plane down the edges of the lid so that it measures about 38 inches long and 16 inches wide.

3. Decorate the side edges of the lid with a pair of 1/2-inch beads (see 11-1 bottom detail).

4. To cut the beaded profile, first select a suitable cutting blade (see 11-17). Set up the plane to cut a bead on the leading edge. After you have cut the first bead, cut a second bead on the face of the board so that the first bead is fully rounded. Finally, adjust the fence and cut a third bead alongside the second (see 11-18).

5. If this procedure is new to you, it's best to practice first on a length of scrap wood. Play around with the plane until you are reasonably confident. Adjust the plane blade so that it makes the very finest of cuts. Always hold the fence firmly against the workpiece (see 11-19).

6. Now use the block plane to skim off the corners of the lid (see 11-20) and to chamfer off the sharp end edges of the boards. Use the gouge to cut the decorative notches (see 11-21).

Finishing and Painting

1. When you have achieved a cleanly worked chest, rub the whole works down with the finest grade of sandpaper, then wipe away the dust.

2. Pour out enough teak oil for a couple of coats, and mix it with a small quantity of burnt umber oil paint to make an orange-brown glaze. Apply an all-over coat of the glaze. Sand the chest when dry, then give the whole chest a second coat.

3. When the glaze is dry, use a wad of aluminum foil to dab and stipple the whole surface with the matte black oil paint. Dip and dab, dip and dab, until you have a pleasing allover texture.

4. Finally, give the whole works another coat of the teak oil glaze.

TIPS

• If you don't have the use of a band saw to cut the curves, you could use a crosscut saw and simply remove the corners of the boards to make a triangular foot hole.

• If you are using two 6-inch-wide boards for the chest ends, you could cut out the handle holes on a band saw, or with a large bow saw or coping saw, before you glue the boards together.

• If you don't have the use of a combination plane, simply angle the edge with the bench plane.

VARIATIONS

• If you want to upgrade this project, you could make it from 11/2-inch-thick rough-sawn oak and omit the painting. Use a plain beeswax finish.

• Instead of using nails for holding the box together, you could use glued pegs.

• Although we have used a simple drop-in lid, you could modify the project and fit the lid with hinges and a lock (see Woodshop Techniques section).

• If you want to use this chest for storing clothes, you could add pieces of wood on the inside ends to cover the handle holes and keep out moths.

Carved Pine Chest

A large, decorative carved pine chest.
Shaped with a plane and spokeshave; jointed with dovetails;
carved with a gouge and knife; waxed and burnished.

The chest has been described as the archetypal primary form of all receptacle furniture. That is to say that not only was the chest once considered to be the most vital piece of furniture, but it is thought that just about all other types—sleeping benches, beds, chest of drawers, and all the rest—were simply specialized variations of the chest theme.

In the seventeenth and eighteenth centuries in Europe and America, the large, decorated chest was considered to be a precious item that had to do with marriage and dowries. Although various communities had their own hope and dowry chest forms—some painted, others decorated with applied wood—the carved chest was considered to be the best. If someone had a lot of money, he would go for a carved chest.

DESIGN, STRUCTURE, AND TECHNIQUE
The chest stands about 20 inches high, not counting the 4-inch-high foot blocks, and is 41 inches wide across the front span of the lid and about 24 inches deep from the front of the nosing to the back of the box.

For this project, you can either make a chest from the ground up and then decorate it with carving, or you can carve a found chest. This is not to say that you should start carving a valuable antique, however; look for a large, common piece such as a pine blanket chest.

We were fortunate enough to come across an old chest that was in good shape except for its bruised and battered lid (see color sec-

tion). The chest appears to be an eighteenth-century piece that was carved sometime at the end of the nineteenth century.

For this project, we will not describe how to build the chest or dovetails; this is described in other projects. We will concentrate here on how to build the lid, and how to do the carving. Also, as we live in an old house that has somewhat damp floors, we decided to construct feet for the chest. The traditional idea is that although the feet become damp, the air flow in and around the feet prevents harm to the chest. The feet are optional, but they are an attractive decorative feature well worth making.

WOOD AND MATERIALS
For this project, we decided to use old pine boards. Once they have been planed on one side, they come out at about 1 inch thick. Note that the materials listed below are for building a lid and feet only.

Fig. 12-1. Working drawing, top and center, at a grid scale of 1 square to 2 inches. Bottom right, 4 squares to 1 inch. Bottom left, 1 grid square to 1 inch.

Fig. 12-2. Design drawing, at a grid scale of 5 squares to 2 inches. Note that the design is more or less symmetrical, with the motif being mirror-imaged on the centerline. The motif needs to be aligned so that the grain runs from side to side.

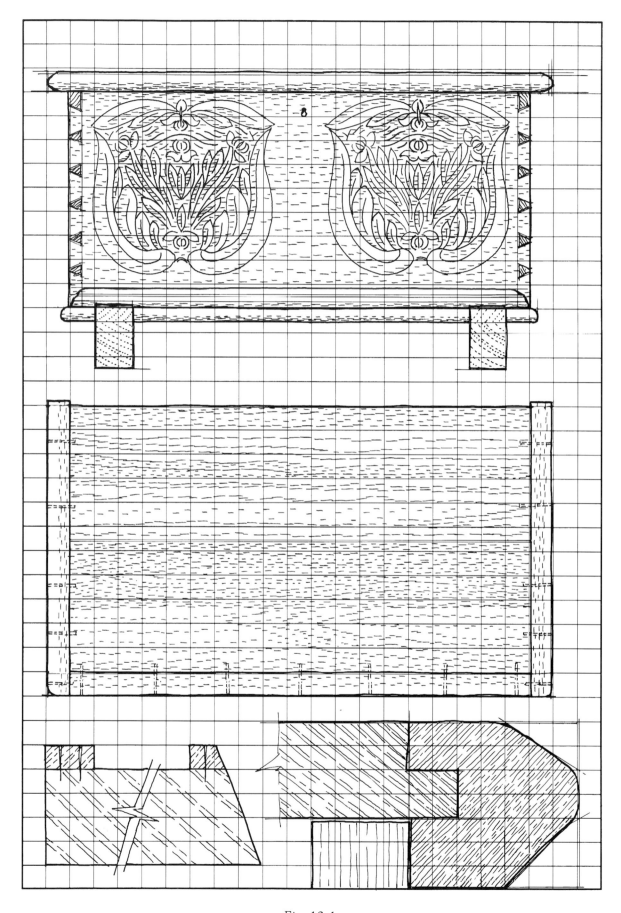

Fig. 12-1

Fig. 12-2

Fig. 12-3. The short length of scrap board clamped alongside the workpiece prevents split-off damage when cutting across the end grain. Note the use of the bench holdfast to secure the work.

Fig. 12-4. Set the workpiece high enough in the vise so that the plane can complete its run without the fence hitting the jaws of the vise.

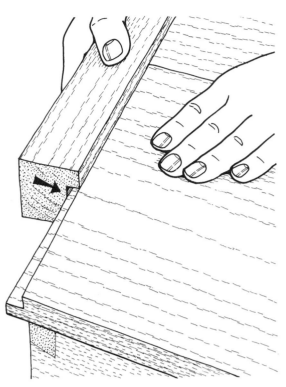

Fig. 12-5. Push the rabbeted step into the groove until the top surfaces of both members come together for a flush and level fit.

For this project you need the following:
• A selection of 1-inch-thick boards at 6 inches wide and at a length to suit your chest.
• A 1³/4-by-1³/4-inch section for the three side nosings of the lid, to suit the size of your chest (see Shaping and Jointing the Lid Nosings, below).
• Two 3-by-4-inch sections for the feet, at a length to suit the depth of your chest.
• Pure beeswax polish.
• PVA glue.

SUGGESTED TOOLS AND SUPPLIES
• An electric band saw.
• A small gents saw.
• A pencil, ruler, and compass.
• An adjustable angle square for marking out.
• A bench drill.
• A marking knife.

Fig. 12-6. Pull the spokeshave like a drawknife.

Fig. 12-7. Aim for a rounded section that rolls around the top and side faces to meet the straight chamfer on the underside.

Fig. 12-8. Cut a tenon on the end of the front nosing to notch into the groove. It's important that the mating faces—the back of the nosing and the tenon shoulder—come together for a good fit.

- A bench plane.
- A small block plane.
- A plough or combination plane with a 1/2-inch blade (we used an old Stanley 45 for the grooves).
- A rabbet plane with a 1/2-inch-wide blade.
- A spokeshave—metal or wood.
- A selection of woodcarving gouges, including a large, straight U-section gouge and a small, bent shallow-sweep gouge.
- A mallet.
- A sloyd knife.
- A selection of sash clamps and G-clamps.
- A sheet of graph paper.
- A sheet of tracing paper.
- All the usual workshop tools and materials, such as sandpaper, dividers, scissors, and brushes.

Fig. 12-9. Slide the side nosing in place on the end board rabbet.

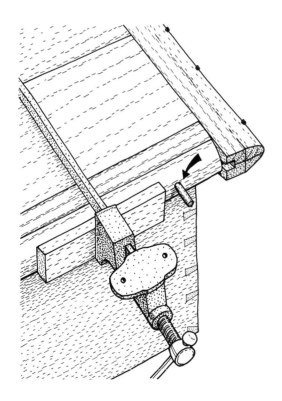

Fig. 12-10. Smear glue on the front rabbet, set the nosing in place, and clamp the whole works up good and tight. Drill holes through the nosing and on into the boards, and fix with glued pegs.

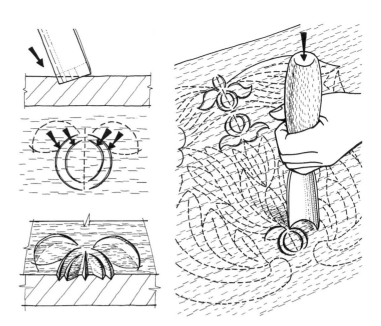

Fig. 12-11. Top left, *angle the gouge so that the resultant crescent-shaped cut is canted back at the edges.* Middle left, *start from the center and work outward. The arrows indicate the angle of the gouge.* Bottom left, *a cross section showing how the contours that go to make up the flower motifs run down into the stop cuts.* Right, *position and hold the gouge with one hand, and give it a single well-placed blow with the mallet.*

CONSTRUCTION
Preparing the Lid Boards

1. After you have made the chest base using the other projects as a guide or purchased an old pine blanket chest of a suitable size, take a good long look at the working drawings (see 12-1 and 12-2) and choose the wood for the lid accordingly.

2. Plane all the boards on one face and both edges, and cut them to length so that the ends are square. The boards need to be slightly over 1 inch longer than the width of your chest to allow for the two 1/2-inch-wide end-of-board rabbets. Pair them up to make up wide boards to fit your chest. As our chest measures about 24 inches from front to back, we needed two boards at about 12 inches wide. Check that all is correct, and then glue and clamp the wood together.

3. When the glue has set, secure one of the

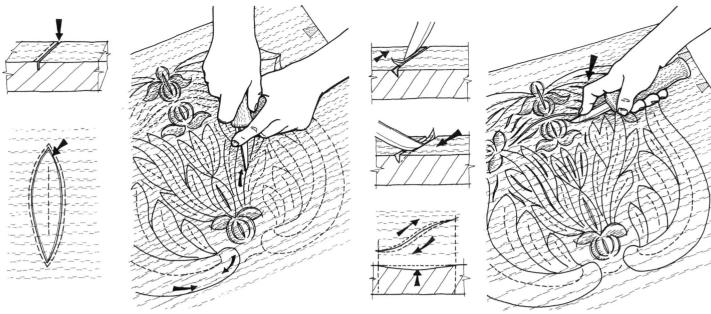

Fig. 12-12. Top left, *sink a stop cut a little to the waste side of the drawn line.* Bottom left, *the narrow band of wood between the stop cut and the drawn line acts as a buffer for subsequent cuts and is cut away at the final modeling stage. The resultant thin bevel catches the light and enhances the modeling.* Right, *hold the knife with two hands in order to make a well-braced, controlled cut.*

Fig. 12-13. Top left, *having first set the central spine line in with a single well-placed straight-down stop cut, make a second at an angle to the first so as to remove a V-section sliver of waste.* Middle left, *make another angled cut on the other side of the stop cut to complete the V-section incision. In almost all instances, the cuts occur at an angle to the grain.* Bottom left, *reduce the cutting pressure at the ends of the motifs so that the cut feathers and tails out at the ends.* Right, *run the knife with a firm dragging stroke. If need be, use both hands to increase the downward pressure.*

boards flat down to the bench, with the best face uppermost and the end hanging well clear of the work surface. Check that all is correct, and clamp a scrap piece of wood at the end of the run.

4   Set both the depth stop and the fence of the rabbet plane at 1/2 inch so that the rabbet step is 1/2 inch wide and 1/2 inch deep. With the cutting spur set down for cutting across the end grain and up for cutting with the grain, make repeated passes across the end of the wood until the step is complete (see 12-3). Repeat this procedure for all board ends and what will be the front edge of the lid.

Shaping and Jointing the Lid Nosings

1.   Next, take the 1³/4-by-1³/4-inch piece of wood that you have chosen for the nosings,

and cut it into three lengths to suit the size of your lid. You need one length slightly longer than the width of the lid, and two lengths slightly longer than the sides (see 12-1).

2.   First check that the best faces of the wood are going to finish up at the top and side of the lid, then label the faces with pencil: "groove side," "top of lid," and "outside edge."

3.   Take the combination plane or plough plane, and set both the depth stop and the fence at 1/2 inch. The 1/2-inch-wide trench should occur 1/2 inch in from the side of the wood (see 12-1 bottom right detail).

4.   Secure the wood in the vise so that the groove side is uppermost and the top of lid side is facing out from the bench, and then run the groove (see 12-4), making repeated passes until you reach the depth stop.

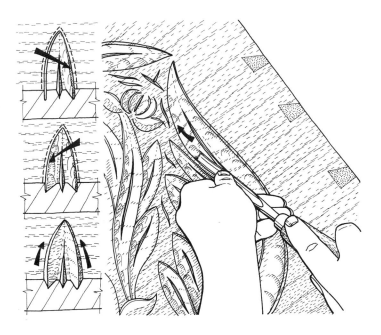

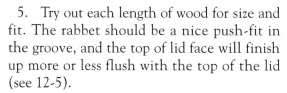

Fig. 12-14. Top left, *cut and carve down toward the edge of the leaf so that the central area is convex and untouched.* Middle left, *now do the modeling on the other side, so that the central area is left standing like a little hillock.* Bottom left, *trim back the edge to leave a delicate chamfer around the motif.* Right, *use a well-controlled two-handed cut, one hand holding and pushing, and the other hand guiding and bracing. Aim all the while to run the blade at a low-skimming angle to the run of the grain.*

Fig. 12-15. *Detail of the modeling.*

5. Try out each length of wood for size and fit. The rabbet should be a nice push-fit in the groove, and the top of lid face will finish up more or less flush with the top of the lid (see 12-5).

6. Mark the wood with all the guidelines that go to make the profile of the nosing (see 12-1 bottom right). This done, secure one of the nosing pieces in the vise with the end angled up toward you, and use the spokeshave to round over the section (see 12-6). Though you would normally push the spokeshave, on this occasion you need to pull it toward you in much the same way as when using a drawknife. Although you could use a drawknife for this procedure, the spokeshave allows for better control of the depth and angle of the cut.

7. Aim for a simple nosing profile, with the outside quarter rounded over so that the top face runs into the side, and with the underside quarter chamfered off at a straight angle. Remove all the corners (see 12-7). Repeat this procedure on the other two lengths of nosing.

8. Take the long piece of nosing that is intended for the front edge, and use the gents saw to cut 1/2-inch tenons on both ends (see 12-8). The best procedure is to cut one end, set it on the front of the lid to mark the length, and then cut the joint on the other end. Aim for a tight push-fit, with square shoulders.

9. Slide the side nosings in place on the ends of the boards (see 12-9)—no glue is used

for the side nosings—then smear glue on the front rabbet and clamp it in place. Having no glue on the end rabbets allows for movement of the lid boards without the possibility of the wood splitting.

10.   Drill, glue, and peg the nosings at the front, corners, and sides (see 12-10). After the glue has set, use the block plane to shape the corners to match the profile.

Laying Out the Motifs

1.   First, study the project photographs (see color section) and the design grid drawings (see 12-2), and note how the motifs are incised and chip carved. Although at first sight the designs give the illusion that they are quite deeply carved—almost reliefs—they are in fact made up from a number of simple, repetitive shallow cuts, and the carving process is a lot easier than it looks!

2.   Enlarge the design to fit the size of your chest, make tracings, and then pencil press-transfer the designs onto the wood.

Setting in and Modeling the Flowers

1.   Start by taking a deep U-section gouge—a 1^1/$_2$-inch-wide number 11—and set in the curved stop cuts that go to make the stylized flowers. Cant the tool over at a slight angle, and aim to sink the cut in to a depth of about 1/8 inch (see 12-11 top left). Repeat this procedure for all the semicircular stop cuts that go to make up the design of the various flowers (see 12-11 middle left). The procedure is as follows: First position the tool on the drawn line. Angle it out slightly from the center of the flower, and then give it a single blow with the mallet (see 12-11 right).

2.   When you are happy with the depth and placement of the stop cuts, take a small, shallow sweep gouge or knife, and slice at a low angle into the stop cuts to create the little sliced-crescent forms that go to make the flowers (see 12-11 bottom left).

Setting in and Outlining the Leaves

1.   Take the knife (we prefer to use a Swedish sloyd knife) and make single cuts slightly to the waste side of the drawn leaf

Fig. 12-16. Detail of the modeling.

outlines (see 12-12). The best procedure for making these sliced stop cuts is to hold the knife in a firm grip, with one hand holding and maneuvering and the other bracing and guiding, and then pull the knife in a slow, dragging stroke at a low angle around the design (see 12-12 right). The key words are control and pressure. Be ready to change the direction of the cut to suit the run of the grain. The line of cut should be about 1/16 inch to the waste side of the drawn line (see 12-12 bottom left).

Cutting the Incised V-Section Sliced Details

1.   If you look closely at the design drawings (see 12-2), you will see that a good number of the forms are made up of sliced V-section cuts. There are sliced cuts at the flower centers, sliced cuts marking out the leaf centers, sliced frondlike cuts used as fillers, and so on. The deepest and widest part of the V-section cut is at the center, with the ends tailing out to shallow points. Study the design and practice these cuts on a piece of scrap wood.

2.   When you are confident about making the cuts, set to work on your chest. With the knife held in one hand and dragged (see 12-13

Fig. 12-17. Saw off the front ends of the foot blocks at an angle, and cut a line of decorative notches across the top front edge. Aim for a swift, bold execution.

right), first set the center of the form in with a single straight-down stop cut (see 12-13 top left) to establish the depth and overall direction of the form. Set secondary cuts on each side and at an angle to the initial stop cut, so as to remove a sliver of waste (see 12-13 middle left). Repeat the three-cut sequence until you achieve a V-section that is at the required depth, width, and shape (see 12-13 bottom left).

Final Modeling

1. Once you have established the design with the gouge and knife, you next contour the surface of the wood in the more relaxed procedure known as modeling. The stop cuts act as brakes or controls. Using a knife or gouge, set to work shaping the contours (see 12-14 right). To model the leaflike forms, first slice at an angle toward the outside edge down into the bottom of the stop cut that defines the form (see 12-14 top left). Work all around the form until the central area is left

standing in high relief (see 12-14 middle left). Then use a knife to slice the edges of the form back to the drawn line (see 12-14 bottom left), and skim to a good finish.

2. Use a straight gouge or a crooked knife to skim the whole design to a surface that is smooth to the touch (see 12-15 and 12-16).

3. Next, fit and fix the lock and hinges (see the Woodshop Techniques section).

4. Finally, wax and burnish the whole chest to a good finish.

Making the Feet

1. The feet can be made to just about any design you like. All you need is a section to keep the chest about 3 to 4 inches off the ground, and stops glued and nailed at the ends (see 12-1 bottom left for runner end profiles).

2. Saw the front ends off at an angle, and run a line of decorative gouge notches across the front ends (see 12-17). Then nail a length of fancy molding across the bottom front of the chest, and the chest is finished and ready for showing.

TIPS

• If you decide to build this chest from scratch, either use 12-inch-wide boards or edge-butt two 6-inch boards and then plane down to a finish. A chest made of wide boards looks much better than one made of narrow boards. Although I glue two 6-inch boards together to make 12-inch-wide boards, I don't glue the wide boards together to make up the total lid width. Having two side boards simply set side by side looks better, and the unglued butt joint allows for movement.

• If you are a beginner to woodcarving, it's a good idea to practice with the tools and techniques on a piece of easy-to-carve wood before you attempt this project. It's also a good idea to read a couple of books on the subject (see the Reading List).

• When modeling the flowers, if you find that your gouge makes rough cuts or has to be bullied into action, your tool may be blunt, the wood may be unsuitable or damp, or you may not be following the procedure correctly.

Barrel-Top Sea Chest

A chest or large box with a barrel lid; the lid is made from tulip polar and salvaged pine floorboards.
Shaped with a spokeshave, knife, and plane; dovetail jointed; glued and nailed; oiled and waxed.

Of all the large chest types, the sea chest is the best known and the most evocative. This is the "pirate's treasure" chest seen in movies and comic books—a large chest with a barrel or humped lid and massive iron straps at the corners and maybe over the lid. The rather mundane truth of it is that most chests of this type were no more than traveling trunks. The idea of the rounded lid was that it shed water, like a roof.

Our chest is in fact part old and part new. When we came across a massive broken and battered chest base with iron corner straps, we felt it was a treasure that deserved to be given a new lease on life.

DESIGN, STRUCTURE, AND TECHNIQUE

The chest is about 34 inches long, 24 inches wide, and 29 inches in total height (see 13-1 and 13-2). The instructions for this project concentrate on making the barrel lid and the cyma curve foot. The working drawings do in fact give you enough information to enable you to make the total chest; if necessary, you can refer to one of the other projects in the book for instructions on building a chest. If you can cut the dovetails for the lid, manage all the planing for the barrel staves, and shape the decorative foot, the rest is easy.

WOOD AND MATERIALS

Note that the materials listed below are for building a lid and foot only. Our chest was made of an even-grained, gold-colored wood, but we don't know the variety. We studied similar chests in museums and decided to make the sides of the lid and the foot from tulip poplar and the barrel covering from old pitch pine floorboards, and then stain and oil the whole works to achieve a matched finish. We felt that a characterless wood like tulip would be easy to stain and match, and the pitch pine would make for a good, strong contrast.

Traditionally, many chests of this size, type, and character were made from cedar or camphor wood. If you are making the whole chest, use a strong, dense, plain-grained wood such as cedar or parana pine. Avoid woods that have a strong odor, exude resin, or have lots of knots. Although a chest of this type needs to present the impression that it is strong, it shouldn't be so heavy that it can't be lifted, so avoid fancy exotic woods like mahogany, and overly heavy woods like English oak.

For this project you need the following:

• Two prepared $7/8$-inch-thick boards at 24 inches long and 6 inches wide for the ends of the lid.

Fig. 13-1. Working drawing, top, *at a grid scale of 1 square to 1 inch and* bottom, *2 grid squares to 1 inch. Note the hidden lapped dovetail joints at the box corners, and the foot rails with their rabbets and hidden lapped dovetails.*

Fig. 13-2. Cutting guide, at a grid scale of 1 square to 1 inch. Note that you will have to cut foot lengths and staves to fit.

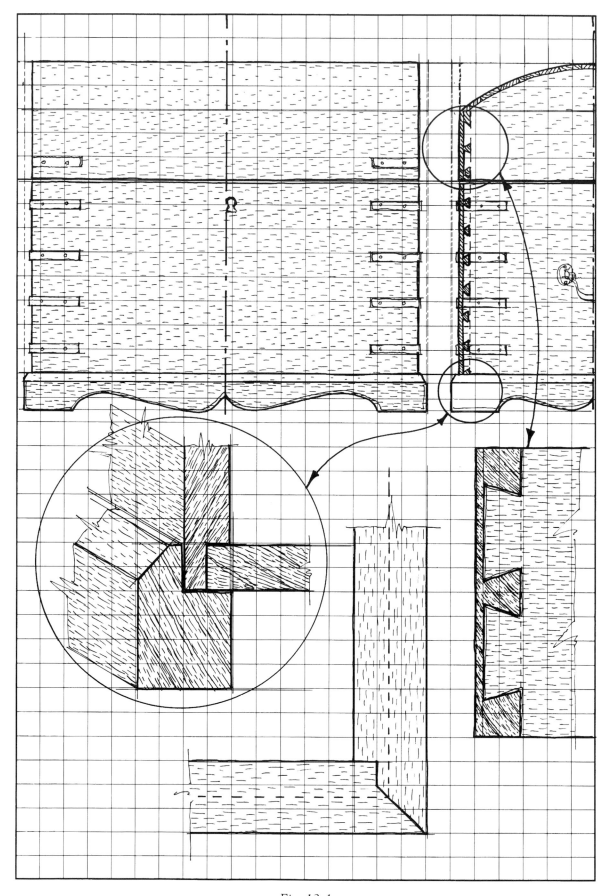

Fig. 13-1

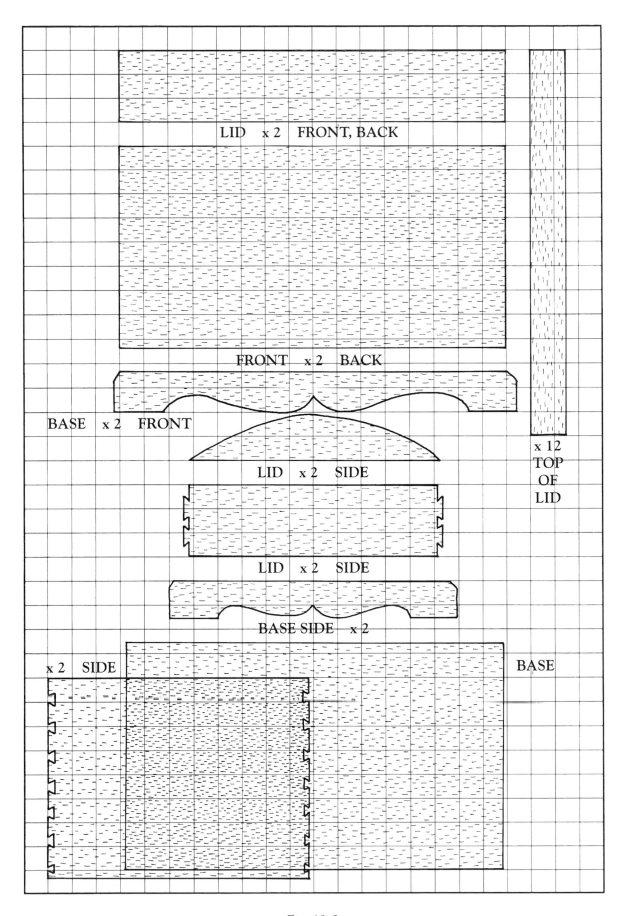

LID   x 2   FRONT, BACK

FRONT   x 2   BACK

BASE   x 2   FRONT

LID   x 2   SIDE

LID   x 2   SIDE

BASE SIDE   x 2

x 2   SIDE

BASE

x 12
TOP
OF
LID

Fig. 13-2

Fig. 13-3. Hold the boards at 90° from each other to make a corner, and then use a blade to transfer the shape of the dovetail through to the end grain.

Fig. 13-5. Secure the workpiece with the hold-fast, and use the mallet and chisel to chop out the waste. Work back from the end grain edge.

Fig. 13-4. Set the workpiece in the vise and use the fine-toothed brass-backed gents saw to cut across the corners. Make four cuts—two to define the flared angle of the cavity, and two to define the straight lines at the neck.

• Two prepared 7/8-inch-thick boards at 33 inches long and 6 inches wide for the long sides.

• Two prepared 7/8-inch-thick boards at 24 inches long and 5 inches wide for the arch former pieces.

• A selection of 7/8-inch-thick boards at 33 inches long and 2 1/2 to 3 inches wide for the barrel staves.

• Two prepared 33-inch-long 2-by-3-inch sections for the long sides of the foot.

• Two prepared 24-inch-long 2-by-3-inch sections for the short sides of the foot.

• Hinges, handles, and a lock to fit (see the Woodshop Techniques section).

• Water stains.

• Danish oil and beeswax polish.

• Nails.

• PVA glue.

Fig. 13-6. Gently pare the cavity back to a good fit.

Fig. 13-7. Hold the chisel flat down against the workpiece and gently skim the base of the cavity down to a flat, level finish.

SUGGESTED TOOLS AND SUPPLIES

- An electric band saw.
- A pencil, ruler, and compass.
- An adjustable angle square or template for marking out the dovetails.
- A marking knife.
- A bench plane.
- A block plane.
- A rabbet plane large enough to cut a 1-inch-wide step.
- A marking gauge.
- A small saw like a gents or dovetail.
- A spokeshave.
- A small bevel chisel at about 3/8 inch wide.
- A mallet.
- A holdfast.
- A sheet of graph paper.
- A sheet of tracing paper.

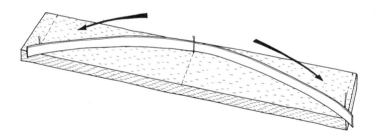

Fig. 13-8. Tap in nails to mark the two ends and the peak at top center, and then bend the strip into place to form a natural bow shape.

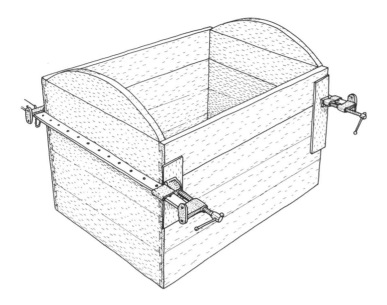

Fig. 13-9. Smear glue on mating surfaces, then put the lid together and clamp it in place on the chest base. Adjust the clamps until the lid is aligned with the base.

Fig. 13-11. Repeatedly plane off a shaving and test-fit until the stave comes to a good fit against the edge of the lid rim.

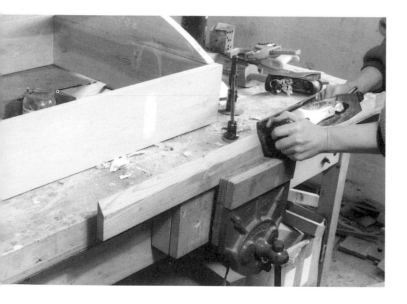

Fig. 13-10. Set the stave in the vise and use the bench and block plane to cut the chamfered angle.

• A selection of bar and sash clamps.
• All the usual workshop tools and materials, such as sandpaper, dividers, and scissors.

CONSTRUCTION

Designing and Cutting the Lid Dovetails

1. Study the project photographs (see color section) and the working drawings (see 13-1 and 13-2). Note how we have built the lid to fit a specific found chest. Although our chest had a foot, we will show you how to make one. Decide whether you want to follow our lead or modify the project and make the whole chest, using other projects for guidance (see projects 11 and 12). Once you have found or made a chest, you are ready to make the lid. First look at the working drawing details and note how we have used hidden or lap dovetails for the joints, with the tails showing on the end boards.

2. Take the two long boards and measure, mark, and cut them to length so that they fit your chest. Use the adjustable angle square or a template to mark out the dovetail. Then use the gents saw and a small, straight chisel to

Fig. 13-12. Glue and clamp the staves in place, nailing and tidying up as you go. Allow a little extra wood at the ends so that you can cut back to a flush finish.

Fig. 13-13. Use the low-angle block plane to cut the arched lid down to a smooth finish. Run the plane diagonally for the most efficient cut.

chop out the dovetails. This is a very easy procedure; just be sure to make all your cuts slightly to the waste side of the guidelines.

3. One piece at a time, secure a short board in the vise and use the first piece to transfer the shape of the dovetails through to the end grain. Aim to have the dovetails stop about 3/16 inch short of the face, so that the joint is secret (see 13-3). Use a knife or chisel to make the marks. Label mating joints with pencil so that you know what goes where.

4. Carefully shade in the areas that need to be cut away, then take the small gents saw and make four cuts across the angle—a cut for each side of the pocket, and a cut each for the guidelines as seen on the inside-box face (see 13-4).

5. With all the primary saw cuts in place and with the workpiece held flat down and secure on the workbench, take the mallet and straight chisel and set to work systematically chopping out the waste (see 13-5). Work slowly back from the board end until you reach the line of the shoulder.

6. Finally, clean out the angles and pare back to a tight push-fit (see 13-6 and 13-7). Repeat this procedure for all four corners of the lid.

Building the Barrel Arch Frame

1. When you have achieved all four straight sides that go to make the lid, take the arch former boards and mark them to size so that they are as long as the inside-box length of the lid ends (see 13-1 top right).

2. Tap nails in at ends and top center, and bend a flexible strip of wood, metal, or plastic into place so as to create a natural bow shape (see 13-8). Adjust the strip so that the inside edge runs through the side and center nails. Use a pencil to make a clean, smooth-curved guideline and then cut out the resultant arch shape.

3. Smear glue on all mating faces of the dovetail joints and the arch-to-end-board butt joints, and clamp up. It's a good idea to clamp the lid in place on the base (see 13-9); then, even if the box and lid are slightly skewed, at least they will come together for a good fit.

Fig. 13-14. Use the block plane and spokeshave to cut the stave ends back to a slightly rounded flush finish.

4.   Drill and spike the arched former board through to the end board, and then leave the whole works until the glue is set.

Marking and Fitting the Barrel Staves
1.   When you have achieved the basic lid frame, then comes the exciting if challenging task of fitting the barrel staves. The first and last staves in line are the most tricky; these staves have to be shaped to fit the long side edges of the lid frame. For the first stave, take a strip about 3 inches wide and at a length to suit your needs, and use the planes to shave it down to a good fit (see 13-10).

2.   The easiest procedure for fitting the first stave is to plane off one edge at an angle, test-fit, shave off a little more wood, test-fit again, and so on, until all mating surfaces are a neat, close fit (see 13-11). When the first stave is cut to size, smear glue on mating surfaces and

nail it in place. To prevent the wood from splitting, you can drill pilot holes for the nails.

3.   Once the first stave is in place, you need to repeat more or less the same procedure for subsequent staves. The only difference is that the board-to-board angle—meaning the edge that you are chamfering to meet the right-angled edge of the one that has gone before—will be acute, but nowhere as sharply chamfered as the first board. Each stave needs to have one edge chamfered off at an angle and one edge left at right angles.

4.   When you have planed the edge of the second stave to fit the first, smear glue on the top edge of the arch board and on mating edges, clamp the two staves together so that glue oozes out of the butt joint, and then secure with oval nails.

5.   And so you continue, planing the individual staves to a good fit, gluing edges, clamping, and nailing, until the barrel-like form begins to take shape (see 13-12). Don't worry about the glue dribbles; simply wipe them off with a handful of shavings, and then move on to the next stave in line.

6.   When you reach a little over halfway—just past top center—change tack and start over from the other edge.

7.   If you work as described, you will reach a point when the whole arch is covered except for a gap that is something less than 3 inches wide. This is perhaps the most tricky step, in that the final stave needs to be chamfered on both edges. Once again, the best way to proceed is to shave off just a little wood at a time and test-fit frequently.

8.   Punch the nail heads below the surface, plug the holes, and wait for the glue to set. Then take the block plane and skim the whole surface down to a smooth, curved finish (see 13-13). Finally, use the block plane and the spokeshave to clean up the edges and corners (see 13-14).

Making the Foot and Finishing
1.   Study the feet in the working drawings (see 13-1), then take the 2-by-3-inch section of wood that you have set aside for the foot, and measure, mark, and cut it to length.

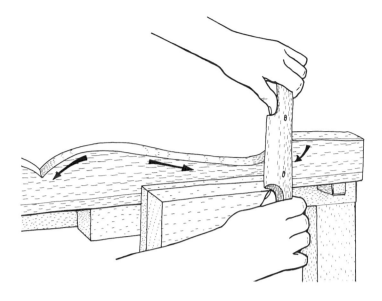

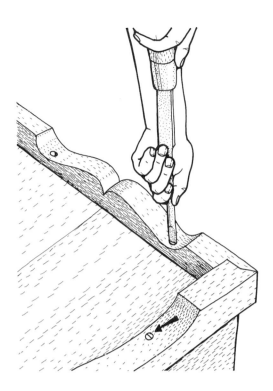

Fig. 13-15. *Make sure that you cut with the run of the grain, from the peaks down into the valleys. Aim for a swift, direct finish.*

Fig. 13-16. *Screw the foot rails in place so that the base is held secure in the rabbet.*

2. Draw the cyma curve to size, make a tracing, and pencil press-transfer the traced lines onto the best face of the wood. Do this with all four lengths that go to make up the foot. Allow extra wood at the ends for the corner joints.

3. Set the rabbet plane to cut a 1-inch-wide, 1-inch-deep step, and run it around the inside top edge face of the wood.

4. Use the bench plane to cut the outside top edge of the wood down to a crisp 45-degree chamfer, as shown in the working drawing detail (see 13-1 bottom left).

5. Cut the cyma curve on the band saw, then use the spokeshave to bring the cut face and edges to a good finish. Be sure to run the spokeshave in the correct direction to the run of the grain (see 13-15).

6. Next, cut a lapped miter or a mitered dovetail for the corner joints, then glue and screw the foot in place around the underside rim of the chest (see 13-16).

7. Use a fine-grade sandpaper to rub the whole works down to a good finish, stain the lid to match the existing chest base, and give all the outside surfaces a coat of Danish oil.

This done, give all surfaces a swift rubdown with a fine-grade sandpaper to clean off the nibs of grain, and then use the beeswax to burnish all the surfaces to a rich sheen finish.

8. Finally, fit hinges and fixtures (see the Woodshop Techniques section), and the chest is ready for storing all your treasures!

TIPS

• If you decide to use salvaged wood for this project, ask the supplier to remove all the nails and to plane one face. Experience has shown us that if the supplier has to plane the wood, he will do a good job of removing the nails!

• As our found chest base already had iron straps at the corners, we decided to have all the lid ironware made to match. It's best if you design the ironware to suit your specific chest. A good blacksmith can help you do so.

• If you plan to use this chest aboard ship, be sure to use waterproof glue throughout.

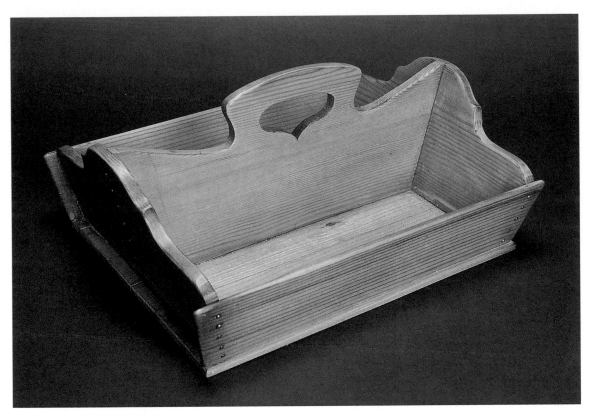

New England Knife Tray

Pennsylvania Book Box

New England Colonial Salt Box

New England Candle Box

New England Pipe Box

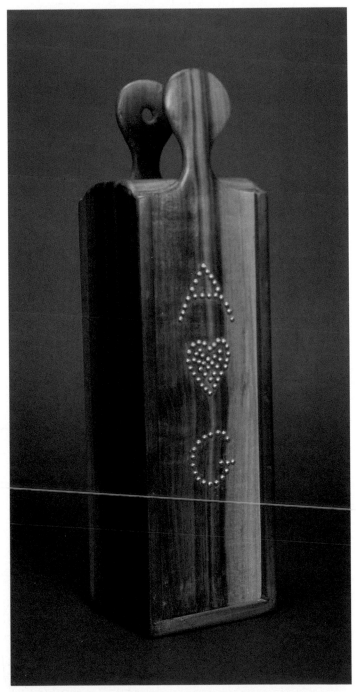

Early American Candle Box

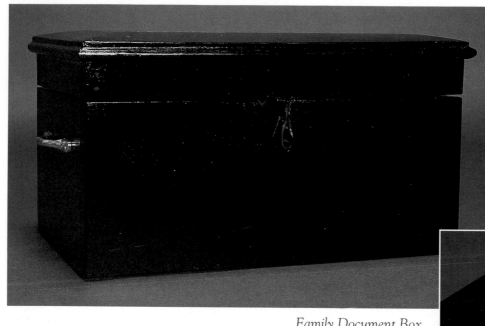

Family Document Box

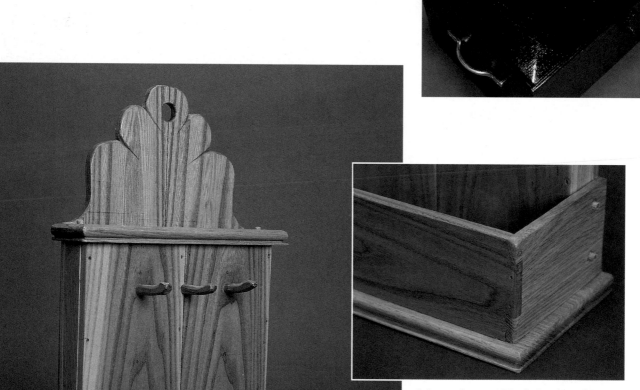

Massachusetts Knife Rack and Box

Pencil Box

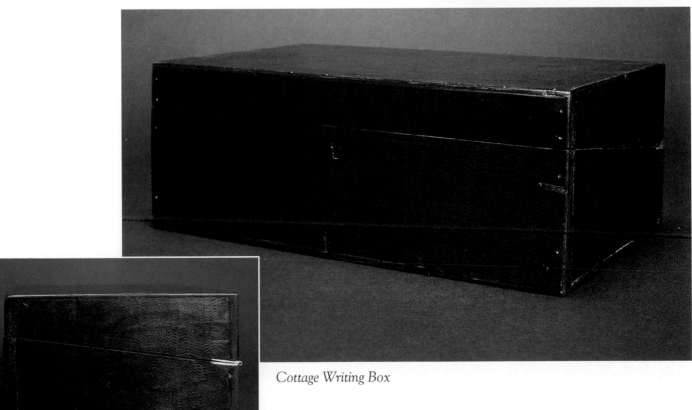

Cottage Writing Box

Six-Board Chest

Carved Pine Chest

Barrel-Top Sea Chest

Painted Pine Blanket Chest

Painted Pennsylvania German Dowery Chest

Painted Pine Blanket Chest

A New York State painted pine blanket chest.
Made from salvaged pine floorboards; shaped with a knife and plane; dovetail jointed,
glued, and nailed; painted and aged.

When the early Americans wanted to make boxes and chests, they were generally limited by their tools, skills, and the availability of suitable wood. When a family wanted a large piece like a blanket chest, they had to either roll up their sleeves and make it themselves or search around for a local furniture maker. As to the shape and design, they might well have had in mind the carved pieces they had seen back home, but with the lack of tools, skills, or suitable materials, the chest usually would be built from an inexpensive wood like pine—sometimes even wood salvaged from another project—and then decorated with painted motifs that echoed the carved furniture of the motherland.

This particular piece draws its inspiration from a blanket chest that was made in New York State around 1825. The museum original is dark green with brightly painted flowers and garlands on the front face.

DESIGN, STRUCTURE, AND TECHNIQUE

The chest is about 27 inches long, 12^1/2 inches wide, and 12^1/2 inches in total height (see 14-1). The body is made from 5/8-inch-thick wood. The lid and base slabs are made from 1-inch-thick slabs, with the edges shaped with a plane. The corners are jointed with through dovetails, with the long front of the chest showing the best face.

We decided at the outset to stay true to the American folk make-do-and-mend traditions of chest making by using salvaged wood throughout. The project picture and detail (see color section) and the painting grids (see 14-2 and 14-3) show how we made the best of rather poor salvaged wood by using wood filler, painting and aging the ground, and then decorating with brushwork. If you have been held back in the past because of the high cost of new wood, or you know where you can get your hands on a stack of old floorboards, this is your chance to make a really beautiful chest.

WOOD AND MATERIALS

As this project is built around the idea of using salvaged boards, we decided to use old house timbers. After a good deal of searching around, we managed to find a supply of pitch pine floorboards. As the building—an old warehouse—was built at the beginning of the nineteenth century, the pitch pine was very appropriate for this copy of an 1825 chest.

For this project you need the following:

• Two 5/8-inch-thick boards at 26 inches long and 10^1/2 inches wide for the two long sides.

Fig. 14-1. Working drawing, top, at a grid scale of 2 squares to 1 inch and bottom, 4 squares to 1 inch. The two details show alternative edge profiles.

Fig. 14-2. Color painting grid, at a scale of 4 squares to 1 inch.

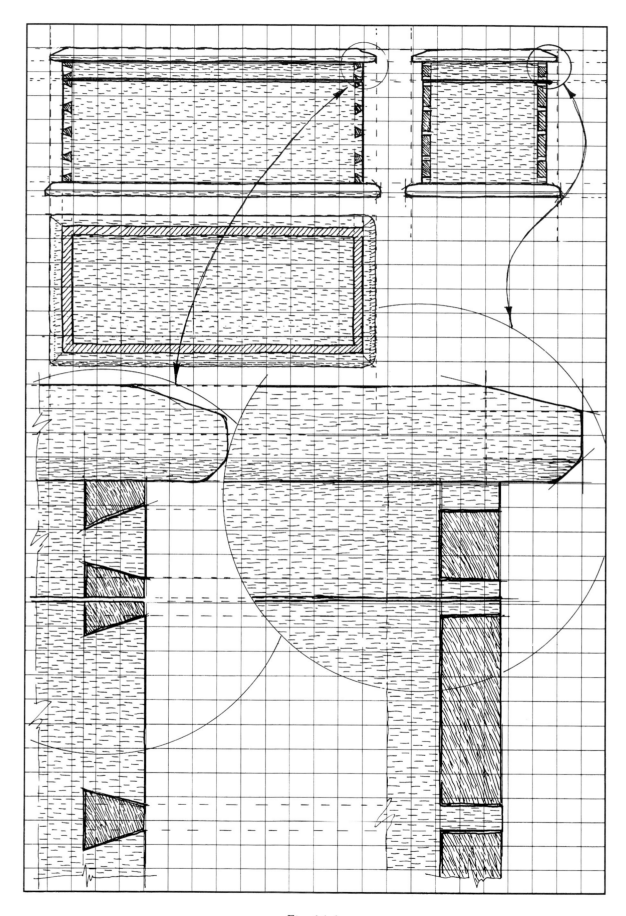

Fig. 14-1

Fig. 14-2

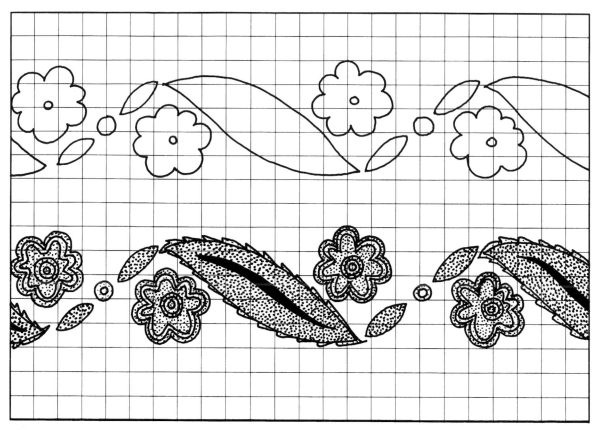

Fig. 14-3. Color painting grid, at a scale of 4 squares to 1 inch. Top, *outline of the motif.* Bottom, *the finished motif with color overlays.*

• Two ⁵/₈-inch-thick boards at 12 inches long and 10¹/₂ inches wide for the ends of the chest.

• Four 1³/₈-inch-thick boards at 7 inches wide and 28 inches long for the lid and base slabs.

• Hinges, handles, and a lock to fit (see Woodshop Techniques section).

• A good selection of acrylic paints.

SUGGESTED TOOLS AND SUPPLIES

• An electric band saw.

• A pencil, ruler, and compass.

• An adjustable angle square or dovetail template for marking out the dovetails.

• A marking knife.

• A bench plane.

• A cutting gauge.

• A small block plane.

• A coping saw.

• A small saw like a gents or dovetail.

• A small bevel chisel at about ³/₈ inch wide.

• A mallet.

• A sheet of graph paper.

• A sheet of tracing paper.

• Fine-point brushes.

• All the usual workshop tools and materials, such as sandpaper, dividers, and scissors.

CONSTRUCTION
Planning and Marking Out

1. Study the project photographs (see color section) and the working drawings (see 14-1). Note how we built the 12-inch-wide base and lid slabs from narrow boards. Sit down and figure out how to best get the box out of your particular salvaged wood. Keep in mind that you might have to modify the working stages to suit your wood.

2. Take the two 26-inch-long side boards, and saw and plane them down to a finished size of 25 inches long, 10¹/₈ inches wide, and ⁵/₈ inch thick.

3. Take the two end boards, and saw and plane them down to a finished size of 12

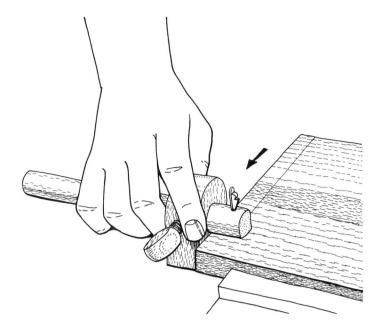

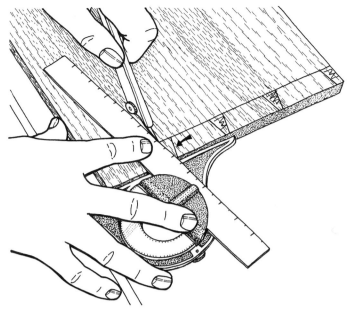

Fig. 14-4. *Use the gauge to run the guidelines. Take care not to cut too deep.*

Fig. 14-5. *Use the point of the knife to mark out the dovetails. To prevent mistakes, first shade in the areas that need to be cut away.*

inches long, 10¹/₈ inches wide, and ⁵/₈ inch thick.

4. Next, saw a 1¹/₄-inch-wide strip from the edge of each board for the lid rim. Label all eight component parts—the edges and the best faces—with pencil so that you will know how they relate to each other.

5. Make sure that all the ends are square and true. Set the gauge to the thickness of the wood, and run a shoulder line around the ends of the board ⁵/₈ inch from the edge (see 14-4). Do this on both ends of all boards.

6. Use the adjustable bevel square or slide bevel to mark out the shape of the dovetails on the ends of the long boards (see 14-5). Shade in the waste areas that need to be cut away.

Cutting the Dovetails

1. When you have clearly marked and shaded in the areas that need to be cut away, set the wood in the vise and use a fine-bladed saw such as a gents to run cuts down to the waste side of the drawn line, so that the saw kerf just touches the scored shoulder line (see 14-6). If you find it easier, you can tilt the

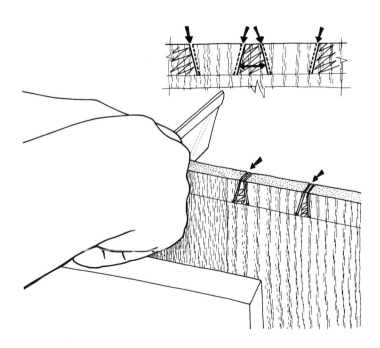

Fig. 14-6. *Top,* run the cuts to the waste side of the drawn lines. *Bottom, use a fine-toothed saw to run cuts down on the waste side of the drawn line, with the saw just touching the line. Some woodworkers prefer to have the work held at an angle so that the cuts are vertical.*

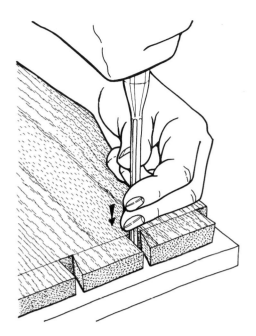

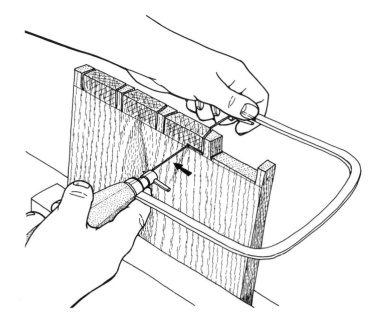

Fig. 14-7. Use the bevel-edged chisel to pare off the waste. Work first one side and then the other.

Fig. 14-9. Saw away the waste by running the saw to the waste side of the drawn lines, then pare back with the chisel.

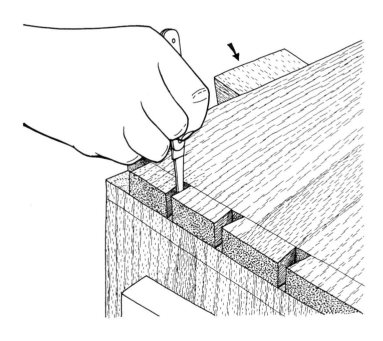

Fig. 14-8. Use the dovetails as a pattern. Place the board for the pins in the vise, and use scrap pieces of wood and clamps to hold everything secure. Use a long-bladed knife or chisel to transfer the pin shapes through to the end of the board.

wood in the vise so that the cuts are vertical.

2. Take the sharp chisel and pare back the waste to the level of the shoulder line so as to separate the dovetails (see 14-7).

3. Now set the end boards in the vise and use the dovetails to mark out the shape and position of the dovetail pins. Use a sharp pointed tool like a penknife (see 14-8).

4. Run starter cuts with a fine-bladed saw like a gents, and then use a coping saw, fretsaw, or bow saw to clear the bulk of the waste (see 14-9). Make sure your line of cut stays to the waste side of the drawn lines.

5. Hone the chisel to a razor-sharp edge, then pare all the joints to a good, crisp sharp-edged finish. Cut and fit all the dovetails on all eight components (see 14-1). If a joint is too tight—a light tap should be all that is needed for assembly—then study the joint to find out where the problem is, and pare the tight place down with the chisel.

6. Test-fit the whole structure to make sure it fits together properly (see 14-10). Aim for a tight push-fit. Cut and joint the lid frame in the same manner.

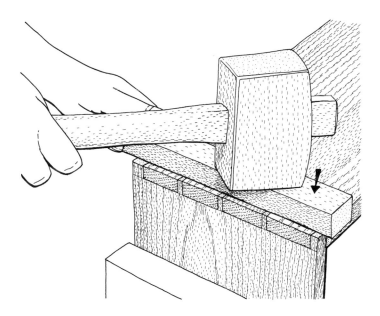

Fig. 14-10. Protecting the workpiece with a scrap piece of wood, lightly tap the joint together.

Fig. 14-11. Space the clamps evenly, one at each end and one at the top to prevent bowing or twisting.

Making the Lid and Base Slabs

1. Before you start work, look at the project photographs (see color section) and the working drawings (see 14-1 top), and note how the base slab has a slightly rounder edge profile and is slightly larger in width and length than the lid slab. All the working procedures are the same for the lid and the base, but the base is slightly heavier and bolder.

2. To make the lid, first plane your wood down to a finished size of $26^{1}/_{2}$ inches long, $6^{1}/_{2}$ inches wide, and about 1 inch thick. If the wood is slightly thicker, say $1^{1}/_{18}$ inches, then so much the better. If you have managed to get wide boards, you can skip steps 2 and 3.

3. Smear glue on mating edges, and clamp the two boards together to form a single slab that is slightly wider than 12 inches (see 14-11).

4. When the glue has set, remove the clamps and clear the bench. Take a look at the working drawing details (see 14-1 bottom left and right), and decide which edge profile you want to use. They are much the same, except the one on the left is slightly wider and more rounded.

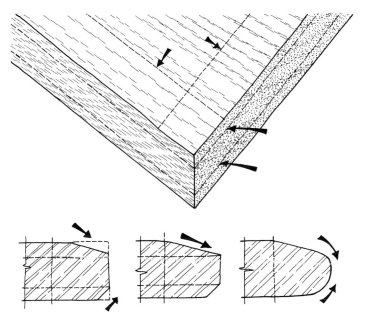

Fig. 14-12. Top, run a $1^{1}/_{8}$-inch-wide borderline around the top face of the lid slab and two guidelines around the edges. Bottom, left to right, knock off the corners, slope the top at an angle and down from the guideline, and round over the sharp edges.

Fig. 14-13. Hold the slab boards in the vise and plane off the sharp corners. Work at an angle to the grain. (Note that Gill has taken one hand away so that you can see what's going on.)

Fig. 14-14. Turn the slab around in the vise and work the end grain edges. Use the block plane to skim off the top angle.

5.   Use the pencil, ruler, and square to run a 1¹/8-inch-wide border around the top face of the slab, a ¹/4-inch-wide border around the underside, and a ¹/2-inch-wide band centered along the edges (see 14-12 top).

6.   Set the slab in the jaws of the vise, and use the bench plane to shape the long side edges and the block plane to shape the end grain edges. The best procedure is to first skim off the sharp corners of waste on top and bottom, reduce the wood on the top edge so as to flatten the angled edges, and then round over the whole form so that the edge profile runs in a smooth line through to the top face (see 14-12 bottom, left to right, 14-13, and 14-14).

7.   Work around and around the lid slab, a little here and a little there, until you have a good, strong edge profile, then place the slab on the lid frame and see how it looks (see 14-15).

8.   When you are satisfied with the edge profile, glue up the lid frame, drill pilot holes through the frame thickness, and nail it in place on the underside of the lid slab. Then use the chisel to sink the recesses for your chosen hinge and lock hardware (see Woodshop Techniques section).

9.   With the lid slab in place, repeat the edge-shaping procedure for the base slab, then glue up the sides, and nail the base in place on the underside of the frame. Carefully cut and fit the hardware. Don't fit the key plate and the handles at this stage; just fit the hinges and the lock and cut the keyhole (see Woodshop Techniques).

10.   Finally, use the block plane and sandpaper to bring the chest to a good finish, rounding over the corners and making sure that the dovetail joints are flush.

Decorating and Finishing

1.   Punch all the nails below the surface, then mix a small amount of filler and fill in all cracks and holes.

2.   When the filler is completely hard, take the finest grade of sandpaper and rub the whole chest down to a smooth-to-the-touch finish (see 14-16). If your salvaged wood is in bad shape, you might need to repeat the filling and sanding several times.

3. Clean up the dust, then give the whole chest an all-over coat of dark green acrylic paint. Go for a muted sage color—a green that is toward the bluish side of the range.

4. Wait for the green ground color to dry, then take fine-grade sandpaper and rub the whole chest down so as to reveal the grain. Concentrate your efforts on the curve of the lid, the dovetailed corners, and around the lock.

5. When you have achieved an attractive worn effect, pencil press-transfer the flower designs through to the front face of the chest, and then block them using a fine-point brush. Lay on the colors in this sequence: light green, dark green, red, white, yellow, and pink. Don't overwork the design; try to achieve a simple, naive look, with some of the images looking as if they have been painted quickly with a loose, easy hand.

6. Sand the whole works again so as to slightly cut through the painted imagery, then fit the handles and the lock plate.

7. Finally, give the whole chest a coat of beeswax polish, and burnish to a dull sheen finish.

TIPS

• If you decide to use old floorboards, ask the supplier to remove all the nails and to plane one side. If the supplier has to plane the wood, he will be sure to do a good job of removing the nails!

• If you are ordering prepared wood, remember that the planing reduces the thickness. So, for example, if you order 1-inch-thick wood planed on both sides, it will be about 3/4 inch thick. Either order thicker wood, or have it planed only on one side.

VARIATIONS

• You can easily modify this project to suit your needs. For example, if you want a larger, deeper chest, simply adjust the board lengths accordingly. You won't need to change the edge profile.

• If you don't want to go to the trouble of making the dovetails, you could go for rabbeted joints.

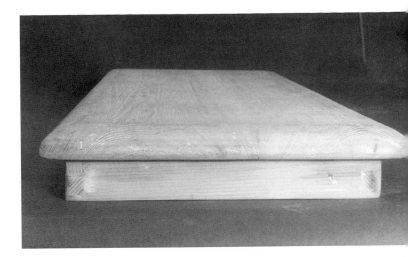

Fig. 14-15. Set the slab on the lid frame and judge how the two elements go together. Try to achieve a good strong profile.

Fig. 14-16. Fill all cracks and holes, and sand the chest in preparation for painting.

Painted Pennsylvania German Dowry Chest

A chest with an applied facade made from salvaged pine floorboards, built up and painted. Shaped with the bench plane and combination plane; dovetail jointed; glued and nailed; painted and aged.

The Pennsylvania dowry chest of the facade-and-tulips type, as made by the German immigrants who settled in America between 1750 and 1850, is surely one of the most powerful furniture forms of all time. With their applied architectural facades and painted imagery, such chests are strikingly dynamic and have long been prized by collectors and enthusiasts. In the late 1920s, collector Henry Francis du Pont paid $44,000 for a single such chest.

Pennsylvania German chests of this type are characterized by having an architectural facade made up of arches supported on capitals and pilasters, a plinth made up of various moldings, and stylized pots of painted flowers.

DESIGN, STRUCTURE, AND TECHNIQUE

The box is about 41 inches wide across the span of the lid, 25 inches high, and 24 inches from front to back (see 15-1).

For this project, we concentrate on how to make the applied facade and how to do the painting, rather than how to make the chest. We decided that the best way to proceed was to look for a good-quality pine traveling trunk made around 1900, and to use this as the basis for the applied work. We set out to do our best to make a copy. We wanted people to be fooled into thinking that our chest is the genuine article—just for a moment, anyway. With this goal in mind, we built, painted, and distressed the chest so that it would look old and much used. If you want to make the entire chest, refer to other projects in this book (see projects 11, 12, and 13).

WOOD AND MATERIAL

As the idea here is to make a replica, we have used old salvaged wood throughout. The wood listed below is only that necessary for the facade and lid of the chest.

For this project you need the following:

- Old salvaged pine floorboards at 1 inch thick and 6 inches wide for the facade and the lid—enough to fit your chosen chest.
- Countersunk slot-head steel screws. (Do not use brass or alloy screws, or Phillips head screws, for this project.)
- Hinges, handles, and a lock to fit (see Woodshop Techniques section).
- Flat or milk paints: matte black, white, green-black, blue, dirty cream or off-white, and a good selection of earth colors.

Fig. 15-1. Working drawing, top, *at a grid scale of 1 square to 2 inches and* bottom, *2 squares to 1 inch. The molding profiles can easily be modified to suit your needs. Make them bigger, smaller, simpler, or whatever. Note that all the elements will have to be sized to fit your own unique box. For this reason, we have only given you the cross-section detail, as shown in the circle insets.*

Fig. 15-2. Painting design, at a grid scale of 3 squares to 1 inch. The design draws its inspiration from a chest made by Johannes Ranck, Jonestown, Lebanon County, Pennsylvania, 1790 (Winterthur Museum, Delaware).

Fig. 15-3. Painting design, at a grid scale of 3 squares to 1 inch.

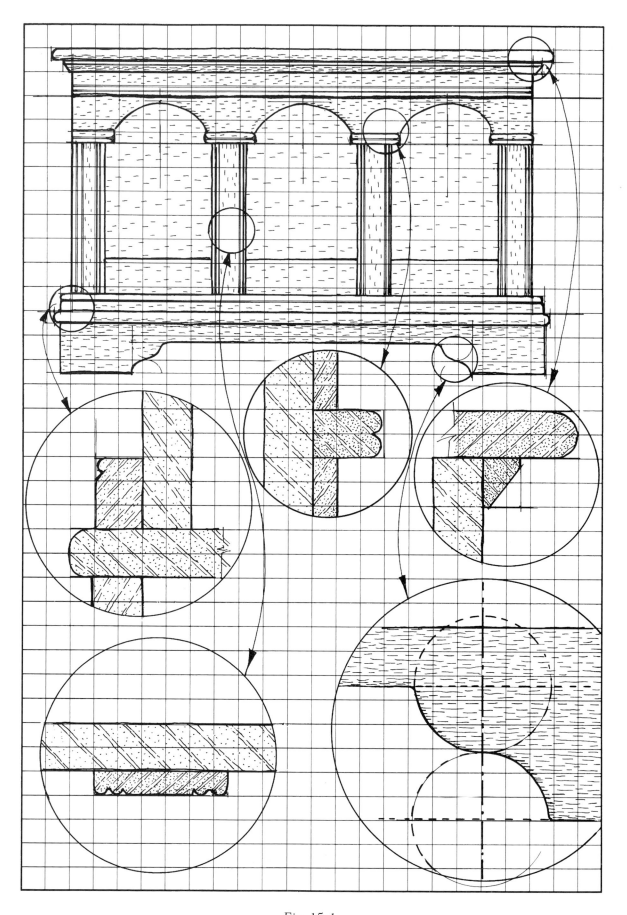

Fig. 15-1

Fig. 15-2

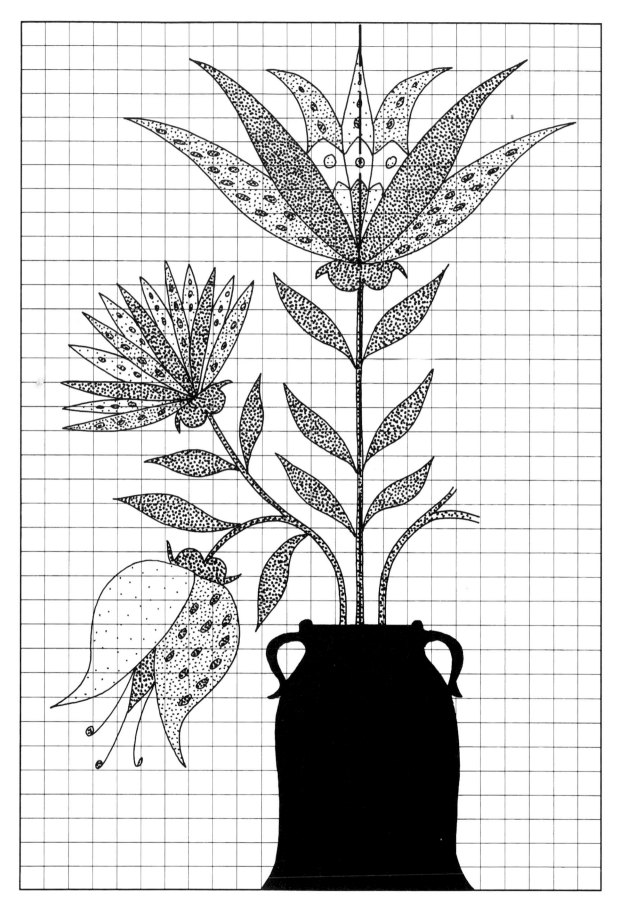

Fig. 15-3

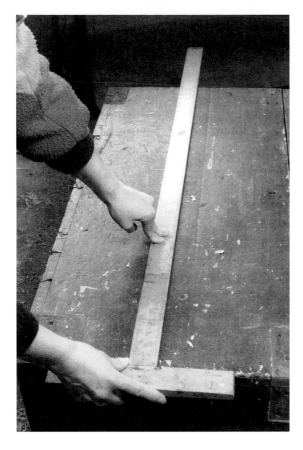

Fig. 15-4. Use a square and measure to assess the potential of your found chest. Modify the designs to suit the size if necessary.

• Old-fashioned tile paint in a muted brick red color as used for floors.
• Beeswax polish.

SUGGESTED TOOLS AND SUPPLIES
• A small electric band saw.
• A pencil, ruler, square, and compass.
• An adjustable angle square for marking out.
• A marking knife.
• A bench plane.
• A small block plane.
• A combination plane (we use an old Stanley 45).
• A spokeshave.
• A coping saw.
• A small saw like a gents or dovetail.
• A flat sander.

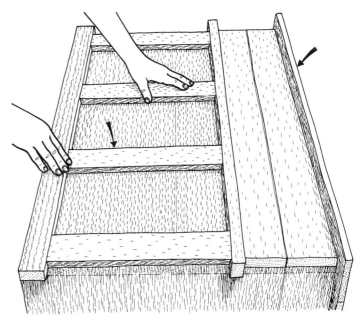

Fig. 15-5. The best way of seeing how the design is panning out is to play around with the size and placement of the component parts.

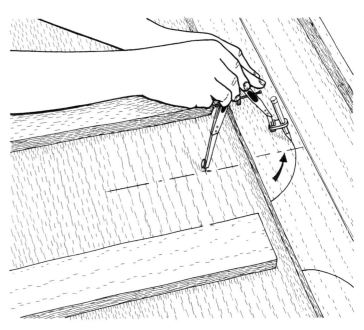

Fig. 15-6. With the point of the compass always set on the centerline, experiment by eye with various radius sizes and circle centers.

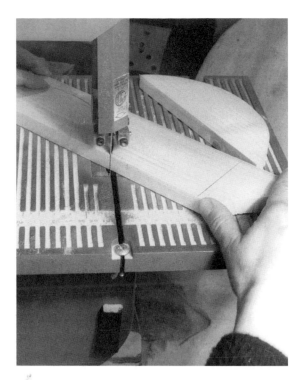

Fig. 15-7. Take care when you cut out the arches on the band saw, as there will be a weak area at the top of each arch.

Fig. 15-8. Set the arch board in place on the chest and see how it fits in with the overall scheme of things. Pay particular attention to the relationship between the arch and the width and thickness of the capitals.

Fig. 15-9. Use your chosen plane to cut the various moldings. Go for big and bold, rather than small and sophisticated.

- A sheet of graph paper.
- A sheet of tracing paper.
- A selection of soft, long-haired watercolor brushes.
- All the usual workshop tools and materials, such as sandpaper, dividers, and scissors.

CONSTRUCTION
Planning and Marking Out

1. Study the project photographs (see color section), working drawings (see 15-1), and painted design drawings (see 15-2 and 15-3). Note how we started out with a common traveling trunk that measured 18 inches high up to the line of the lid, 38 inches wide across the front, and 24 inches deep from front to back, with a 3-inch box lid that took the total height up to 21 inches. Apart from the metal corner straps, this box was entirely flush faced on all sides—no beadings, overhangs, or trim. You probably won't be able to find an identical chest, but do your best to get one with similar overall dimensions.

2. Once you have purchased or made such a chest, lay it on its back and spend some

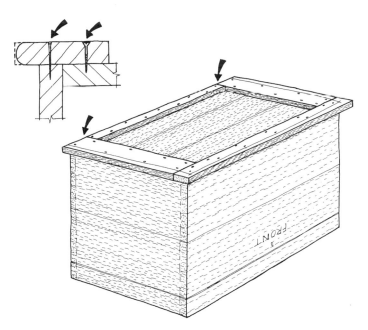

Fig. 15-10. Set the plinth strips in place on the base, check the overhang, and secure with nails and screws. Note that the strip at the back edge needs to be flush with the back of the chest.

Fig. 15-11. Use the block plane to shape the sawn ends to match the molding. Be careful that you don't run into the nail and screw heads.

time assessing the proportions of the front panel (see 15-4). Draw the designs, modifying them to fit your chest.

3. Saw and plane the wood down to the overall thickness and width, as shown in the working drawings (see 15-1). Aim for 1-inch-thick boards for the lid, 1-by-1-inch wood for the pillar capitals, and 1/2-inch-thick wood for all the other front boards. Don't worry at this stage about the foot and plinth. Arrange the wood on your chest and see how the various primary elements relate to one another (see 15-5).

4. When you have made decisions as to board widths, cut all the elements to length, and then have another fitting. While you are at it, temporarily nail the boards to the top of the lid, and use the block plane to swiftly round over the front and side edges.

5. Use the ruler and square to mark in the position of the capitals, then take the compass and draw the three arches on the top board. Be sure to have the compass point on the center line, and pass the pencil line through the top corner of the capitals and

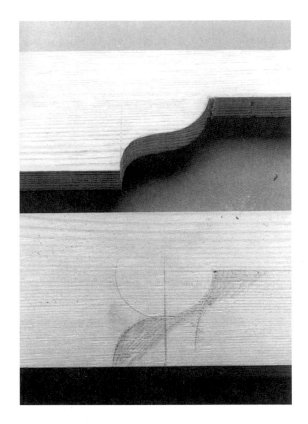

Fig. 15-12. Draw in the width of the skirt, divide the remainder in half to obtain the radius, and then scribe out the two half circles. Use the half circles to achieve the cyma curve shape.

Fig. 15-13. *Having run screws down through the skirt and nailed the corners, reinforce the corners with glue.*

Fig. 15-14. *Take off all sharp edges with the spokeshave. Work with the run of the grain, downhill from high to low wood.*

bring it to within 1/2 inch of the lid line. Play around with various compass settings until you achieve what you consider is an attractive arch curve (see 15-6). Draw this curve on both outside arches, and if necessary, vary it slightly to fit the central arch.

6. When you are satisfied with the shape and position of the arch curves, cut them out on the band saw (see 15-7) and test-fit (see 15-8).

Planning the Moldings and Fitting the Plinth

1. If you study the total project, you will see that this chest is characterized more than anything else by its decorative profiles, or moldings. The lid has a round nosing, the strip under the lid is chamfered off at an angle, the board running across the front of the lid has a single beading, the capitals are double beaded, the pilasters are double beaded on both edges, the foot strip is beaded, and so on—everything is fancy. To cut these pieces, you need either a combination plane or a collection of molding planes. We use an old Stanley 45 throughout. (We have discovered that many old tools—antiques even—are a good deal less expensive than their modern counterparts.)

2. Cut all of the various strips to length and plane them to a good, smooth finish on all sides and faces. Now comes the fun task of planing the moldings. It's best to plane all the moldings at this stage. The procedure is always more or less the same, as described fully in other projects: You select and fit one or another of the blades, set the stop to fix the depth of the cut, set the fence to fix the distance between the edge of the workpiece and the molding, and then make the cut. The main problem with running moldings on thin wood is how best to secure the wood while it is being worked. The difficulty is how to allow for the thickness of the fence runner when the stock is, say, only 1/2 inch thick. The best solution is to set the workpiece up on a strip of waste so that it is raised up off the bench by the depth of the runner, and then hold it secure with the bench holdfast (see 15-9).

3. When all of the moldings have been planed, the next step is to attach the plinth strips (see 15-10). All of the strips but the one at the back, which should be flush, should have an overhang of about 1¼ to 1½ inches. Position them on the base slab and secure with nails and screws (see 15-10 top left). Have the front strip running right across the width, the back end of the side strips stopping flush with the back of the chest, and the back strip tucked in so that it is completely flush.

4. Round over the front end-grain ends of the side strips with the block plane so that they follow through with the front profile (see 15-11).

Making and Fitting the Bracket Foot Board

1. The foot board lifts the chest both literally and figuratively. The board makes the chest special. All that said, the board is wonderfully simple to make. The curves are easy to construct, and the corner joints are lapped and butted. Take the 1-inch-thick floorboards, and plane and cut them to size, leaving the back face unplaned and rough, as old chests have rough surfaces in hidden areas. The boards need to be 4 inches wide (see 15-1).

2. To mark out the bracket foot, run a line about 1½ inches down from the top edge, fix the length of the foot with the pencil, ruler, and square, and then use the compass to set out the two half circles that go to make the fancy curve (see 15-12 bottom). Make allowances for the fact that the front feet need to be slightly longer than those at the side.

3. Cut out the curve on a band saw, bow saw, or coping saw, and then swiftly trim off the rough edges with a plane (see 15-12 top).

4. Position the foot boards so that they are set back about ½ inch from the edge of the plinth nosing, butt-joint the corners, and secure with glue, nails, and screws. Run the screws through the 1½-inch-deep skirt of the top board, so that they are countersunk by about ½ inch. Cut cubes of scrap to fit closely into the corners, and puddle them in glue (see 15-13). If these blocks show a waney edge, then so much the better, for authenticity's sake.

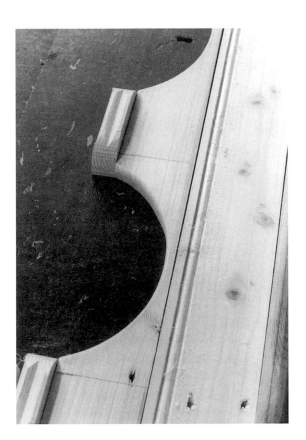

Fig. 15-15. Position and fix the three elements that go to make the top of the arches. All the old nail holes will need to be plugged with whittled and glued pegs.

Fig. 15-16. Drive the nail heads below the surface of the wood. To prevent the wood from splitting along the line of the short grain, you can drill pilot holes for the nails.

Fig. 15-17. The assembled chest, with the false lid, facade, and foot.

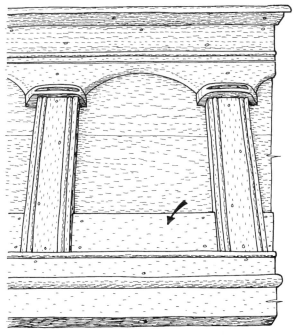

Fig. 15-19. Nail on the filler strip to reduce the height of the panel.

Fig. 15-18. Test the lid and round over the top edge of the arch board.

5. Finally use the spokeshave to cut the sharp edges down to a slightly rounded finish (see 15-14). Screw the lid in place with hinges.

Assembling the Facade

1. Once the foot board is in place, it's time to assemble the facade. Start by gluing and nailing the lid board, the arch board, and the four little capital sections (see 15-15).

2. Fit the molding strips just above the plinth (see 15-16), and then cut and fix the pilasters for a tight wedge fit (see 15-17).

3. Fit molding strips just above the side plinths, making sure that the top edges don't impede the lid (see 15-18). Then fit the small filler strips between the pilasters (see 15-19), punch all the nail heads below the surface, and sand rough areas.

Fig. 15-21. *Concentrate on the areas that would naturally have become worn. Make sure to give the underside edges of the feet a suitably worn appearance.*

Fig. 15-20. *Sand through the surface of the paint at all natural areas of wear. Sand off all sharp corners and edges. Use a fold of hand-held sandpaper to stroke the worn areas to a smooth finish.*

Painting and Finishing

1. When you are pleased with the overall look of the facade, next comes the exciting task of painting. Consider what might have happened to an old chest over its lifetime. At its making, it would have been filled, given several undercoats, and finished with a top coat. Ten years or so later, after the chest had been knocked about a bit, it would likely have been given another swift coat of paint or varnish, and so on for the next hundred or so years. The layers of paint would in fact record changes of fashion and products. Begin by giving the chest an undercoat of matte black, followed by white, green-black, and blue, then a good, solid all-over coat of old-fashioned tile floor paint mixed with paint thinner. (If you prefer, you can choose different

Fig. 15-22. *Aim for a confident, if naive, effect, with all the colors at the muted and earthy end of the range.*

Fig. 15-23. Finish up with the dot-and-dash details. Let the brush make its own characteristic marks.

Fig. 15-24. Use a fine-grade sandpaper to abrade the paint and give it a worn look.

colors for the layers.) Between coats, give the paint some rubbing down and scraping to simulate the wear that would naturally have occurred.

2. When the top coat is dry, take the sander and give the whole chest a rubbing down. Pay particular attention to the raised areas of the moldings, the leading edges of the lid, and the areas around the front side corners (see 15-20 and 15-21).

3. Paint the three panel areas a dirty cream or off-white. Allow to dry, then pencil press-transfer the traced imagery from 15-2 and 15-3 onto the wood.

4. Working from the base color up, block in the big shapes, then pick out the dotted texture, and so on (see 15-22 and 15-23). Go for thin washes of muted earthy colors. Avoid

pastels and all colors that look overly strident.

5. When the paint has dried, rub it down with sandpaper so as to break through at wear areas. In the normal course of things, the inside edges of the panel would be protected from wear, so concentrate your efforts on the panel centers (see 15-24).

6. Finally, give the entire box another good rubbing down with fine-grade sandpaper, lay on a generous amount of beeswax polish, then burnish to a good finish (see 15-25).

TIPS

• You can easily modify this project to suit your needs. For example, you can apply the facade to a made or found chest, you can go for a chest of a different size, or you can make more basic moldings.

Fig. 15-25. Lay on a generous amount of natural beeswax polish, so that there is a slight buildup of hard wax in all the corners and crevices, then use a lintfree cloth to burnish the wax to a high-shine finish.

- When you are planing the wood, aim for a swift, direct finish. You don't want the surface to look machined; it's much better if you can see ripples and undulations, as left by hand tools.

- Don't be tempted to cut the moldings with a power router. If you do, they will look too smooth and altogether wrong for this piece.

- Save any old fittings and replace them just before painting, so that there are age-old deposits of paint in screw holes and over screw heads.

- If you are not sure how much to distress the chest, take a trip to a museum and look at some authentic ones. You will soon see that whole family histories are recorded in the finish of these chests—burn damage, insect attack, curious mends with bits of strap iron, water damage, unfortunate paint-overs with unsuitable colors, and all manner of scuffs and scars.

- When distressing the chest, you could add to the wear on the underside of the feet by lifting the chest up by one handle, and then dragging it across a concrete floor. This will give the underside ends a really good, natural rounded-over effect.

Inspiration Gallery

Box and chest designs all have their beginnings in ideas and notions that have gone before. What usually happens when the woodworker is looking for fresh design ideas is that he visits libraries, buys a few more old books, spends days in museums and galleries, goes to woodworking stores and shops that specialize in antique tools, visits the lumberyard, and so on—all the while taking photographs, making sketches, and becoming absorbed in the project. Finally, having reached a point where he is talking, eating, and sleeping the project, the design solution invariably presents itself, all fresh and shiny. Of course, the research is good fun, and it's wonderful to get to see old boxes and chests, but whoever said that success is 10 percent inspiration and 90 percent perspiration certainly knew what he was talking about!

The gallery presented here is designed to cut out a bit of the legwork and give you a few ideas to help you on your way.

Oak cutlery tray. England, 1760 to 1850. Note the elegant ogee curves that form the handle.

Oak cutlery boxes. North Wales, 1770 to 1830. Boxes of this type and period are characterized by the fretted and pierced back board and tapered shape.

Fruitwood and beech spoon rack and box. England, 1830 to 1880. Designs of this restrained character are common throughout England and America.

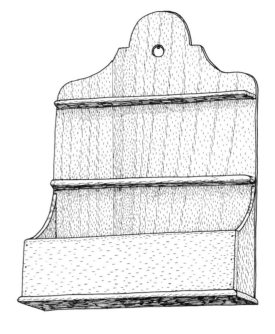

Salt boxes. *Left*, oak with beautiful dovetails showing at the front joints. England, eighteenth century. *Right*, box with painted red and black fern design. Netherlands, early nineteenth century.

Spoon rack and cutlery box. England, eighteenth century. Standing about 25 inches high, this box is special in that there is a secret compartment for valuables with access from a sliding back panel.

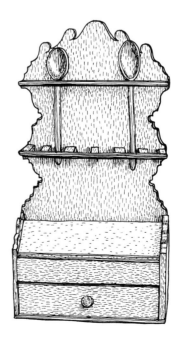

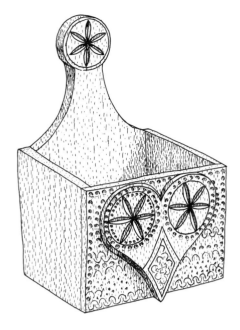

Spill box. Connecticut, eighteenth century. This little box, with its chip carved rounded motif, almost certainly draws its inspiration from English boxes and chests of the same period. Note how the heart shape has been applied.

Wall boxes. England, eighteenth century.

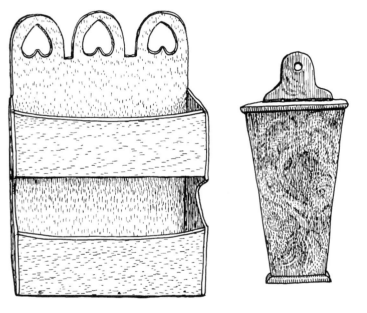

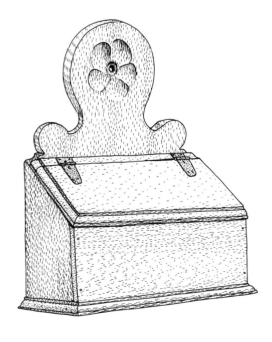

Wall box. New England, eighteenth century. Small flap hinges and a stylized carved flower motif.

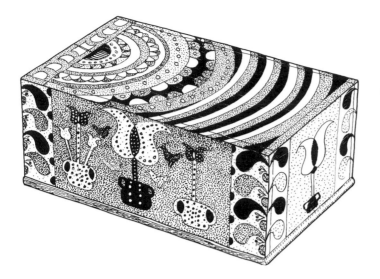

Candle box. Early American, Pennsylvania. Painted with traditional tulip, vase, and heart motifs. This box has a sliding lid so that the lid could be opened and closed without damaging the candles and tapers.

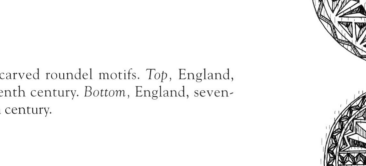

Chip carved roundel motifs. *Top*, England, thirteenth century. *Bottom*, England, seventeenth century.

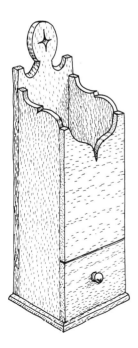

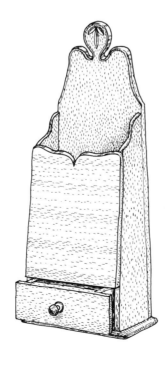

Pipe boxes. *Left*, New England, nineteenth century. *Right*, New England, eighteenth century. Boxes of this size and character were generally designed specifically for holding all the items that had to do with smoking. The long-stemmed clay pipes fit in the top box, and the little drawer held the tobacco.

Desk box. Lancaster County, Pennsylvania, 1825. Painted with compass-worked hearts and flowers.

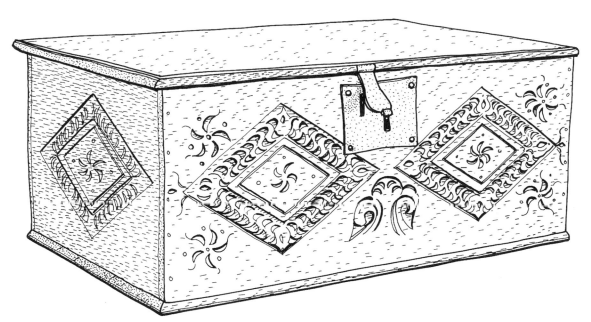

Oak chest. Made in England between 1640 and 1730. Decorated with characteristic carved lozenge motifs. This box is unusual in that there are two secret drawers underneath the interior till.

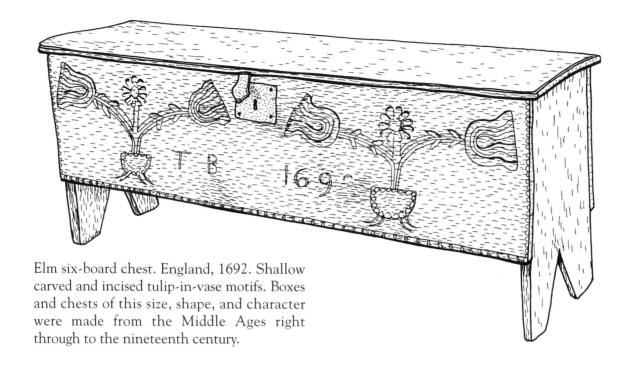

Elm six-board chest. England, 1692. Shallow
carved and incised tulip-in-vase motifs. Boxes
and chests of this size, shape, and character
were made from the Middle Ages right
through to the nineteenth century.

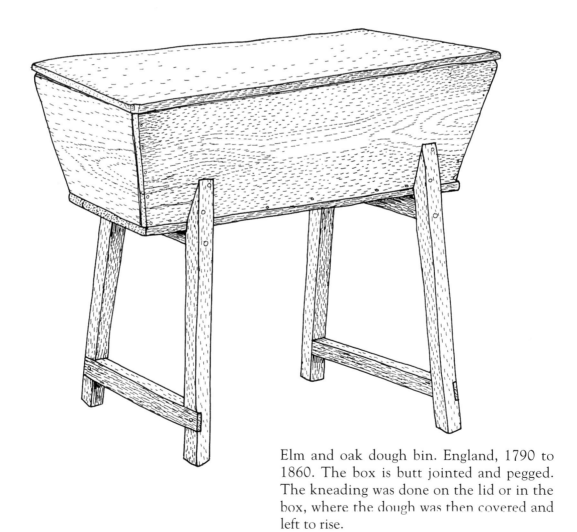

Elm and oak dough bin. England, 1790 to
1860. The box is butt jointed and pegged.
The kneading was done on the lid or in the
box, where the dough was then covered and
left to rise.

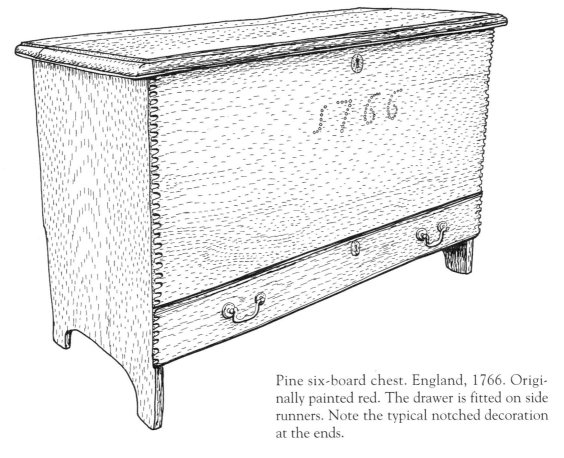

Pine six-board chest. England, 1766. Originally painted red. The drawer is fitted on side runners. Note the typical notched decoration at the ends.

Carved and stained oak chest. Dorset, England, 1650 to 1670. The stylized tulips and compass-worked decoration are mostly incised, with some shallow chip carving and gouge-cut strapwork. There is evidence of red, black, and white stain or paint.

Central panel detail from an oak chest with drawers. England, 1713. Relief-carved birds and flowers with the initials F. N.

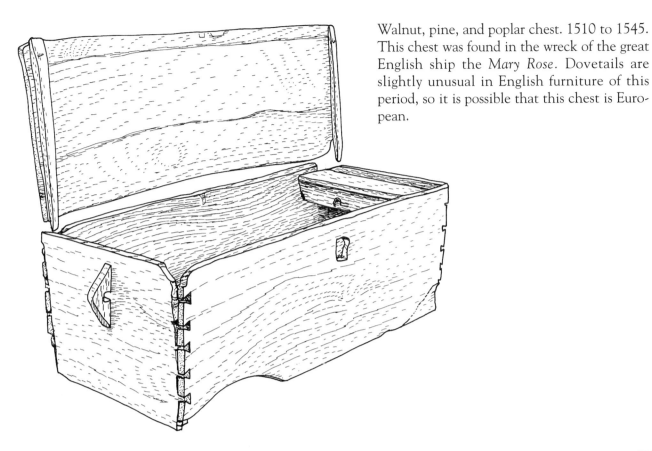

Walnut, pine, and poplar chest. 1510 to 1545. This chest was found in the wreck of the great English ship the *Mary Rose*. Dovetails are slightly unusual in English furniture of this period, so it is possible that this chest is European.

Painted pine chest. England, 1850 to 1900. The chest has been given an all-over coat of brown on yellow to imitate oak, the interior is lined with paper, and the inside of the lid is decorated with a nautical picture. Note the long hinges and the shaped and bolted handle blocks.

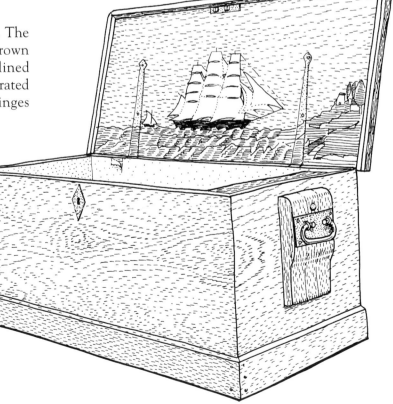

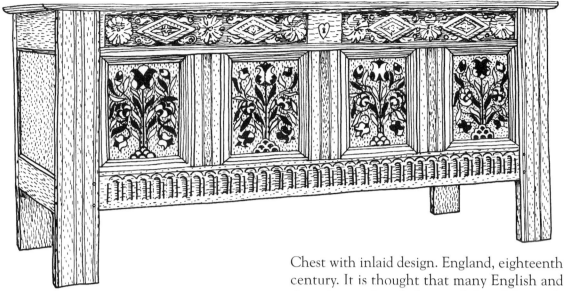

Chest with inlaid design. England, eighteenth century. It is thought that many English and American painted chests of the eighteenth and nineteenth centuries drew their inspiration from early inlaid work. Note the molded beadings and the stylized tulip and vase motifs.

Dowry chest made by Christian Selzer. Pennsylvania, 1784. This chest has all the elements that make Pennsylvania work so special: fine dovetails, a generous footboard with curved ends, bold painted panels with tulip and vase motif, and lots of color. *(Henry Francis Du Pont Winterthur Museum)*

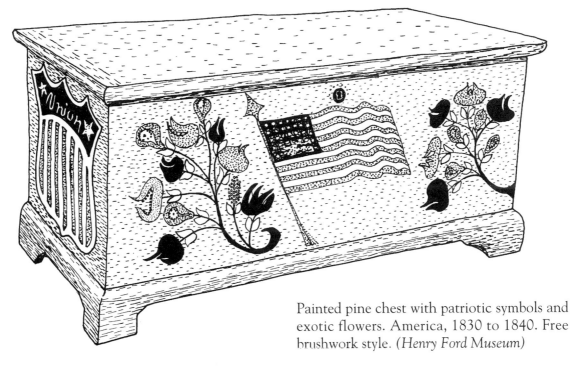

Painted pine chest with patriotic symbols and exotic flowers. America, 1830 to 1840. Free brushwork style. (*Henry Ford Museum*)

Chest. Pennsylvania, 1774. Chests of this early period characteristically are made of hard yellow pine, with the sides and lid constructed from single board widths, and have ball feet. Note the applied arched facade.

Painted pine panel from a large chest. Berks County, Pennsylvania, 1790. The traditional symbols on this panel have their roots in ancient European myths. The crown symbolizes authority, and the horse and rider signify virility. *(Henry Francis Du Pont Winterthur Museum)*.

Woodshop Techniques

BAND SAW

A power-operated saw consisting of a metal band running over and driven by wheels—a good tool for cutting out fancy curved profiles. This saw is ideal for small sections and medium cuts.

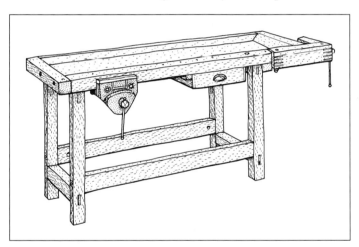

BENCH

Box and chest makers need a good, strong bench fitted with a vise. The bench depicted here has an integral tail vise, a pair of sprung steel dogs or stops, and a quick-release vise. If you are a beginner, get the best you can afford. Avoid benches that rock.

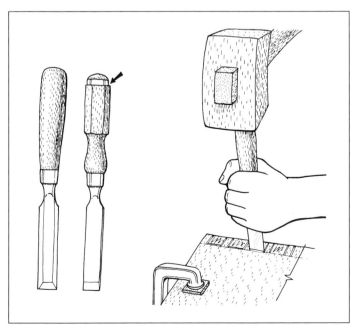

CHISELS

The bevel-edged chisel, *left and right*, is perfect for light paring and for chopping out joints.

The firmer chisel, *middle*, is designed for general-purpose work. A metal ferrule prevents the handle from splitting.

CLAMPS

If you enjoy making small boxes, get plenty of clamps. Always buy the best you can afford; "bargain" clamps can fail catastrophically. C-clamps and G-clamps are screw devices used for securing the workpiece when it is being worked or glued. The C-clamps are used on the underside to draw the boards together, while two G-clamps prevent the boards from rising and buckling.

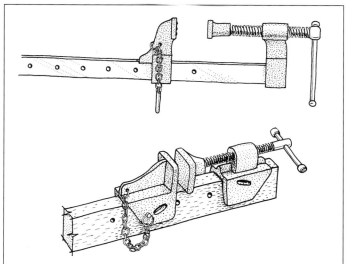

The sash clamp, *top*, is characteristically made up of a bar with a sliding shoe at one end and a screw head at the other. Clamping sets, *bottom*, are a good idea, as they can be used on a variety of bar lengths.

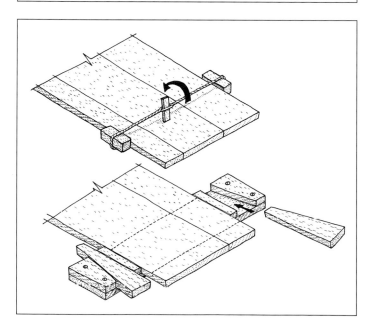

Clamping

A homemade rope-and-twist arrangement, *top*, is a traditional method of clamping up. Note the use of small blocks to prevent the rope from doing damage to the edges of the workpiece. In use you would need to put a heavy weight on top of the boards to keep them from rising and buckling up.

A traditional wedge clamp, *bottom*, is good for small bench work, such as when you are making relatively small boxes.

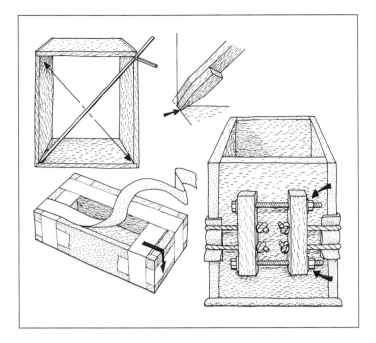

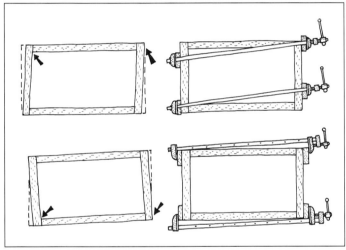

Top left and right, just prior to clamping, test for squareness by using a homemade diagonal rod. Set the rod across the diagonals, first one way and then the other; the box is square when the two measurements are identical.

Bottom left, small boxes can be clamped with strips of masking tape.

Bottom right, a good traditional clamping device can be made with an inexpensive arrangement of bolts and rope. This setup is ideal for clamping massive chests.

Left top and bottom, often the box will be found to be askew and off square.

Right top and bottom, it is usually possible to bring the box into line by judiciously arranging the clamps and blocks.

Designing

To make working drawings, you need a drawing board with a true left-hand edge and a smooth face, a T-square for drawing horizontal lines, and a triangle for drawing vertical lines. Although you can use all manner of fancy high-tech drawing equipment, the traditional board-and-squares kit is by far the most inexpensive, flexible, and dependable.

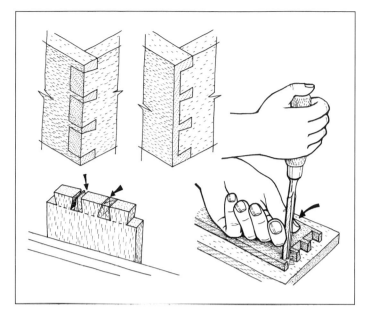

DOVETAIL JOINTS

Dovetails are basically wedge-shaped tenons that fit into wedge-shaped mortises. Traditionally—before the use of modern glues—they were considered to be the strongest joints for box and chest structures, and they are the most attractive.

Top left, the through or open dovetail, in which the ends are visible on both sides of the joint.

Top right, the lapped dovetail, used when you want to have one clean or best face.

Bottom left, use a tenon or gents saw, coping saw, and chisel to cut the waste from around the dovetails.

Bottom right, pare the waste from between the pins.

DOVETAIL TEMPLATES

The size and proportion of the dovetails needs careful consideration. Before beginning construction, you should make a template.

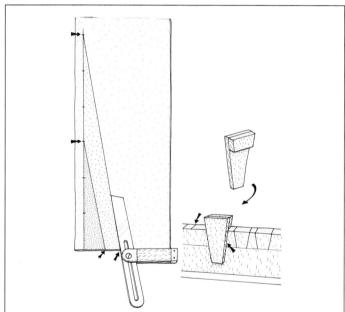

Left, to find the angle, take a right-angled card, and mark it out with six 1-inch step-offs along the vertical axis and one 1-inch step-off along the horizontal. Join up at 2 in 6 to achieve the slope used by nineteenth-century box and chest makers. The smaller 1 in 3 arrangement gives us the slope used by modern woodworkers.

Right, a dovetail template, made from wood. To use the template, first mark out the spacing on the board edge, then hold the template against the mark and draw in the angled shape.

DRILL BITS

Forstner drill bits have long been considered to be the best tool for boring holes. Modern Forstner drill bits are capable of producing clean-sided, flat-bottomed holes. They are particularly useful for boring overlapping holes.

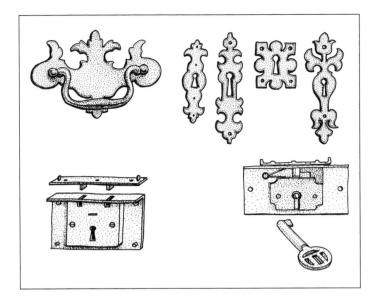

FITTINGS

Generally speaking, all hardware—hinges, locks, and such—are termed fittings.

Top left, characteristic eighteenth-century brass chest handle.

Top right, fancy keyhole escutcheons, as found on early dowry chests.

Bottom left, cut box lock. The lock is cut and recessed into the front at the top center, with the plate being recessed and screwed into the lid.

Bottom right, a small box lock known as a half mortise.

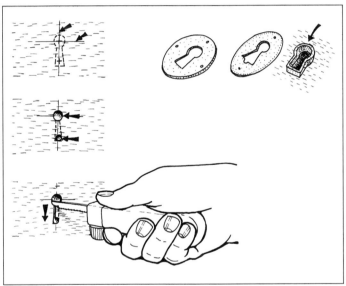

Fitting Locks—Keyholes

Top, establish the position and shape of the keyhole. Make sure that the hole is aligned square with the box.

Middle, drill out two holes to clear the bulk of the waste.

Bottom, use a keyhole saw to join up the holes.

Top right, brass escutcheons, which are designed to protect the keyhole from damage, make for a good finish. They may be nailed over or driven into the keyhole.

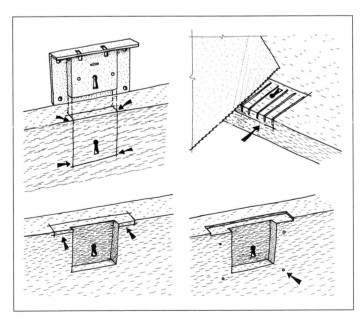

Fitting Locks—Lock Body

After the keyhole is cut comes the task of fitting the lock body or box.

Top left, use the actual lock to transfer the shape of the recess through to the inside face of the chest.

Top right, run a number of saw cuts at an angle across the area of waste, then use the chisel to pare out the recess.

Bottom left, use the lock body to establish the size and position of the recess.

Bottom right, clear the waste with a chisel, and drill pilot holes for the fixing screws.

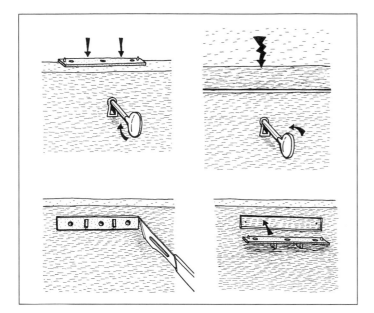

Fitting Locks—Link Plate

After you have fit the lock body, the next step is to fit the link plate on the lid.

Top left, set the link plate in place and turn the key so that the two component parts are locked together. Note the two small spurs.

Top right, push and bang the lid down so that the spurs make alignment marks.

Bottom left, position the link plate so that the spurs are located in their holes, and mark around the edge of the plate with a knife.

Bottom right, lower the recess with a chisel, then run pilot holes and screw the plate in place.

FRETSAW, OR SCROLL SAW

The fretsaw, sometimes called a scroll saw, is the perfect tool for cutting joints and curves in small section wood. If you enjoy making small boxes and are considering getting a fretsaw, be sure to get one that has an adjustable bed. The Draper saw is particularly useful in that it takes both superfine blades and heavy-duty pin-end blades.

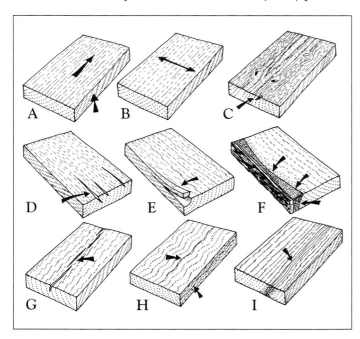

GRAIN

Grain may be compared to a river that flows and undulates through the wood. Box and chest makers need to know about grain characteristics.

(A) The grain direction—its flow and undulation—can be seen on the face and edge of the board.

(B) Across the grain means across the flow or run of the grain.

(C) Avoid wood that has extreme distortions or knots.

(D) End splits can be a problem when the wood starts to dry out.

(E) Loose areas, known as cup shakes, that follow the curve of the annual rings need to be cut away.

(F) Any soft bark and waney edges need to be cut away.

(G) Deep cracks, known as shakes or checks, indicate that the wood has dried out too rapidly. Such wood is best avoided.

(H) Wavy grain, typically found in European walnut and ash, is visually attractive but structurally weak.

(I) Reaction wood has compressed rings that may cause problems when the board starts to shrink.

Grain Problems

An otherwise beautiful piece of wood may show fungal or insect damage. Use such wood with caution.

Wood with both hard and soft grain can be a problem to finish. The soft grain sands out more rapidly, resulting in undulations across the surface.

A plank taken from the heart of the tree, as shown by the annual growth rings, might well warp excessively when it dries out.

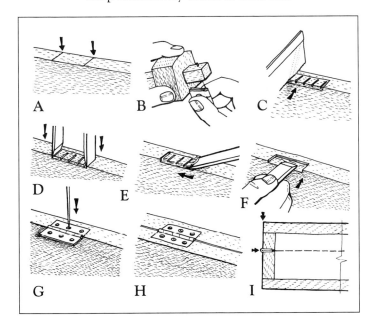

HINGES

Fitting

(A) Decide on the position of the hinge and use the square to mark out its length.

(B) Take two measurements with the gauge—the width and the thickness of the hinge. Make sure that the point is aligned with the center of the pin.

(C) Use a dovetail or gents saw to cut across the area of waste.

(D) Use a chisel to make straight-down cuts at the ends of the recess.

(E) Cut the waste out with the chisel.

(F) Pare the bed down to a smooth finish; aim for a slight slope to allow for the extra thickness around the knuckle area.

(G) Run a pilot hole in at the center and fix with a screw.

(H) Repeat the above procedure so that both flaps are fitted with a single screw at the center.

(I) Check that the lid opens and closes smoothly, make slight adjustments as necessary, and then fit the other screws.

Butt Hinges

Butt hinges, *top left,* are fine for small boxes and chests.

Bottom, left and right, in this instance the hinge is placed with the central pin exactly at the edge of the box, so that there will be a minimum of strain when the lid is opened and closed. Here the whole thickness of the hinge is recessed into the part of the box that has the most wood, with the upper flap of the hinge screwed directly to the face of the lid.

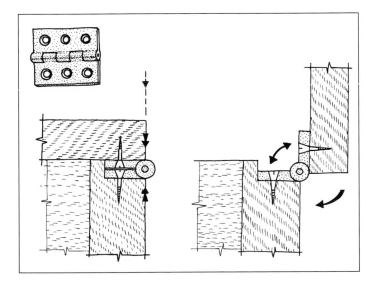

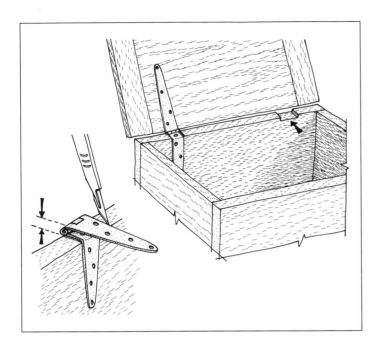

Strap Hinges

Most large boxes and chests are fitted with long strap hinges, either specially forged to shape or store bought and modified to fit.

Left, mark around the hinge and then use a saw and chisel to sink the recess.

Right, sink the recess on the top edge of the back board, and then screw the other side of the hinge to the underface of the lid.

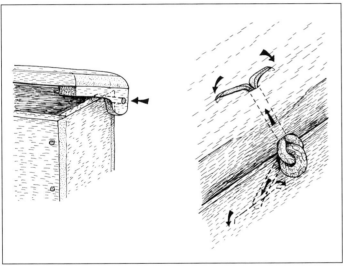

Traditional Hinges

Left, wooden pin hinges, as found on chests and boxes from the twelfth century to modern times.

Right, a cotter-pin or staple hinge, used in the seventeenth, eighteenth, and nineteenth centuries. Hand-wrought round-section iron is looped and one loop is passed through the body of the chest and another through the lid. The loops are linked, with the ends clinched into the wood. Hinges of this character are only suitable for use on massive oak slab chests, where there is little risk of the wood splitting.

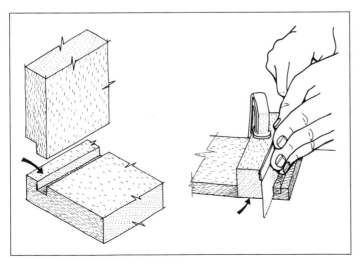

HOUSING JOINT

The housing joint is commonly found on all kinds of boxes and chests.

Left, the narrow strip of cross grain is weak, so this joint is best fixed with glue rather than nails.

Right, when cutting a housing joint with a brass-backed handsaw, clamp a piece of waste alongside the channel. The wood helps keep the saw true and also controls the depth of the cut.

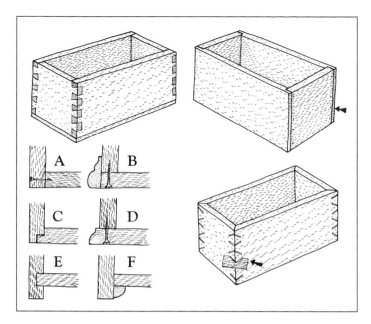

JOINTS

The through dovetail, *top left,* is both strong and attractive—perfect for box and chest making.

Though the lapped rabbet, *top right,* is one of the simplest of all joints, its strength relies primarily on the fixings—nails, screws, pegs, or glue.

Bottom left, (A) plain nailed butt joint, *(B)* screwed butt joint with cover-up moldings, *(C)* rabbet joint, *(D)* screwed butt joint with integral molding, *(E)* housing joint, *(F)* butt joint with glued block.

Mitered joints, *bottom right,* reinforced with veneers glued into kerfs.

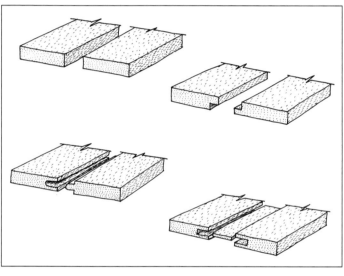

JOINTING BOARDS

Box and chest makers often need to edge-joint boards to make a greater width.

Top left, plain butt jointed.

Top right, rabbeted and reversed joint.

Bottom left, matched tongue-and-groove joint.

Bottom right, grooved and fitted with a loose tongue strip.

MALLET

Every box and chest maker needs a mallet. We use a couple of block mallets for general woodworking and a couple of shaped-head mallets for carving. When knocking a joint together, avoid bruising the wood by using a piece of scrap between the mallet and the workpiece.

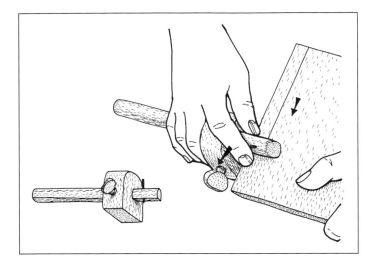

MARKING GAUGE

The single point gauge is used for marking lines that are parallel to the edge of the wood. In use, the gauge is held with the thumb pushing forward and the fingers pushing down and in toward the edge of the board. A common mistake is to place the index finger too near the thumb—it should be pressing downward against the fence and the screw.

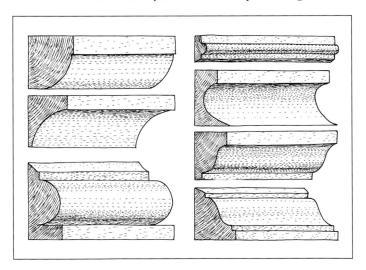

MITER BOX

A sawing guide used for cutting at right angles and 45 degrees; good for making small boxes.

Top, to use the miter box, clamp the workpiece in place and use a tenon saw to make the cut. Hold the saw upright so as not to damage the slot, and use a piece of scrap wood underneath the workpiece to avoid cutting into the base.

Bottom, some boxes are fitted with slots set at right angles—good for sawing small bits of batten and trim.

MITERED EDGE JOINT

The band saw is a great tool for cutting edges at a mitered angle. In use, the bed of the saw is tilted and adjusted to the required angle. The wider the blade, the more accurate the cut.

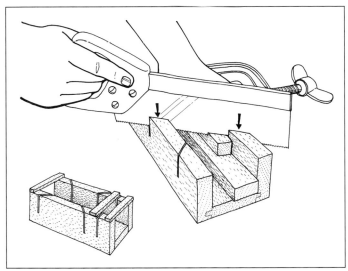

MOLDINGS

Fancy cross sections that are cut on strips of thin trim or directly onto the edges and corners of boxes. The traditional names relate to ancient Greek and Roman stone-carved originals.

Left, top to bottom, ovolo, cavetto, torus.

Right, top to bottom, astragal, scotia, cyma recta, cyma reversa.

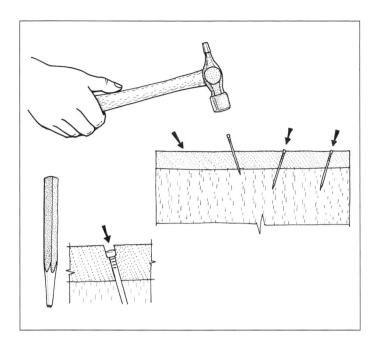

NAILED JOINTS

Many types of boxes and chests are traditionally fixed with nailed joints.

Top, a good technique is to run the nails in at an angle, so that they form a "dovetail."

Bottom, use a nail set to drive the heads below the surface of the wood, and cover them with filler or glued wooden pegs.

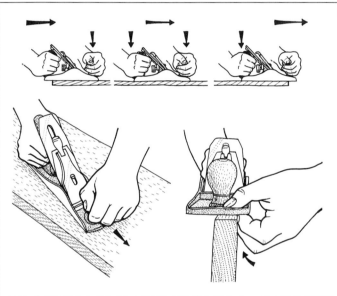

PLANES

A bench plane is a general-purpose plane.

Top, left to right, to prevent rounding over the board at the start and finish of the run, press down on the front of the plane at the start of the stroke, maintain an even pressure through the stroke, and press down on the back of the plane at the end of the stroke.

Bottom left, hold the plane at a skimming angle when cutting face wood.

Bottom right, to plane the edge, clamp the workpiece in a vise, and use the pressure of your thumb and fingers to hold the plane against the wood.

A block plane is best used for small-scale work and for working end grain. The blade is set at a very low angle. A piece of scrap wood helps to prevent split-off damage at the end of the run.

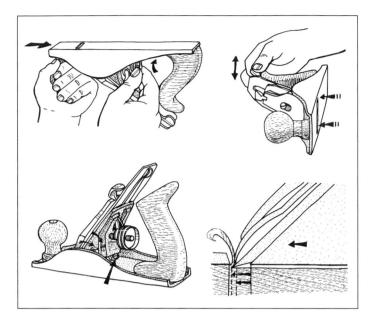

Plane Adjustment

If the plane chatters or makes a scratched cut, or fails to make a cut, the blade needs to be adjusted.

Top left, if the cut is too deep, hold the plane upside down and at eye level, and turn the depth-of-cut wheel counterclockwise to draw in the blade.

Top right, if the blade only cuts at one corner, move the lateral adjustment lever away from the corner that is failing to cut.

Bottom left, the width of the mouth is adjusted by first loosening the two screws that hold the frog, then turning the screw under the depth-of-blade wheel, and finally retightening the two frog screws.

Bottom right, the blade is best set with a narrow mouth for hardwoods and smooth cuts, and a wide mouth for softwoods and coarse cuts. Think of a big mouth as being coarse.

Planing End Grain

The block plane is designed with a low-angled blade—perfect for cutting end grain.

Top, work from end through to center to prevent splitting off the side grain.

Bottom, a slight bevel made with a chisel will also help prevent grain split-off.

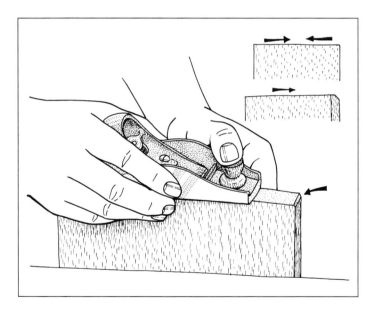

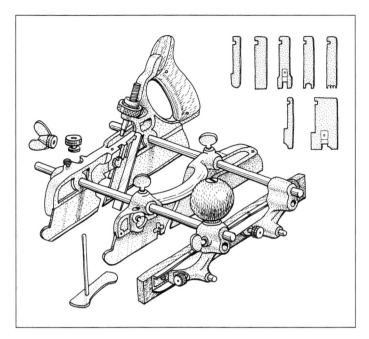

Planing Moldings

If you enjoy making boxes and chests, look for a combination-multi-type molding plane. We feel that our plane—a Stanley 45, made in the United States in 1929—is by far the best tool for the task. It is the perfect tool for cutting fancy profiles. Though they stopped being made about 1960, there are plenty of them around secondhand. Although such planes are currently sold as antiques, they are greatly superior to comparable modern tools and are much less expensive. The planes come with all manner of cutter shapes—fluting, plough, tongue, beadings, reeding, and so on.

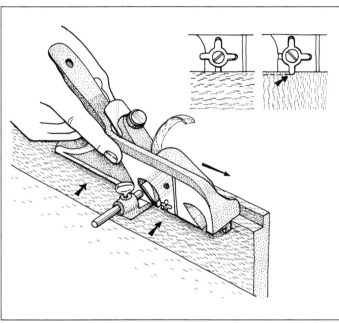

Planing Rabbets

Box and chest makers need a rabbet plane. Note how this model has two seating options for the blade.

Top right, the spur is set *up* for cutting with the grain, and *down* for cutting across the grain. To cut with the grain, start by making sure the spur is up and the fence is set as shown.

SAFETY GUARDS

Most modern machines are fitted with safety guards. Though our photographs often show us working with the guard up, this is only so that you can see what's going on. Always follow safety procedures when using machines.

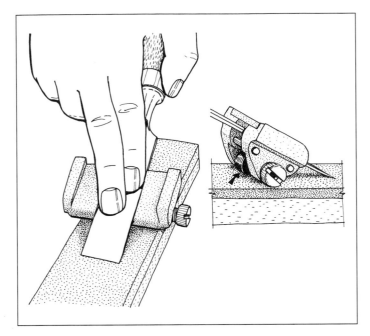

SHARPENING

Chisels and Planes

A honing guide is a great piece of equipment. In use, the blade is first run backward and forward, then finished with a dragging stroke.

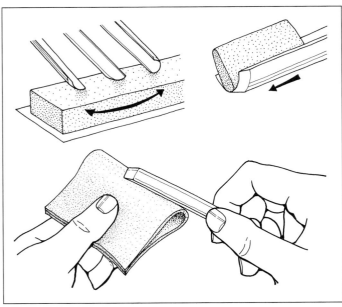

Gouges

Top left, hone the tool with a slow, rolling side-to-side action, so that the whole bevel becomes shiny.

Top right, use a shaped slip to clean out the burr, or wire, from the inside curve of the blade.

Bottom, use a fold of leather dressed with crocus powder to strop the blade to a high-shine finish.

SANDING

By Hand

A good technique when sanding by hand is to glue a sheet of sandpaper grit side up to a plywood base board, and then move the workpiece rather than the sandpaper.

With a Power Tool

A vibrating power sander is a great tool for working large flat surfaces. For safety's sake, fit the machine with a dust bag or have a dust vac set alongside.

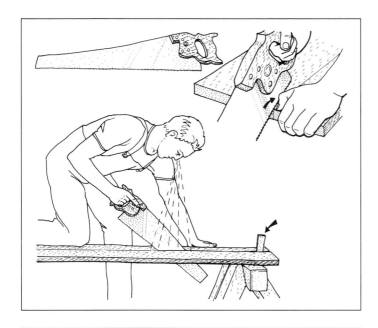

SAWING

Top right, to start a saw cut, hold the saw at a low angle, so that the blade is slightly to the waste side of the drawn line, rest the knuckle of your thumb beside the saw for the first few strokes, and then start the slot with a dragging action.

Bottom, make sure that the blade is vertically aligned with the line of cut—the saw and your shoulder should be in the same plane—and then keep the kerf, the cut made by the saw, open with a small wedge as the cut progresses.

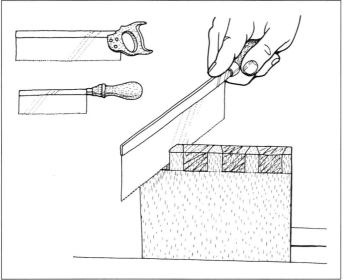

SAWING JOINTS

Top, a tenon saw is best for large joints.

Middle, we use a fine-bladed gents saw for delicate cuts.

Bottom, always run the line of cut slightly to the waste side of the drawn line.

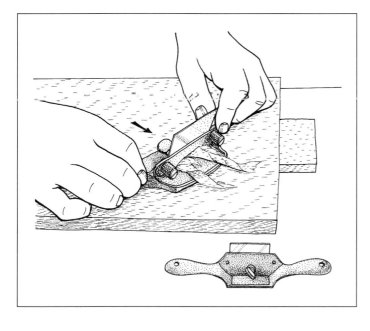

SCRAPER

Double-Handed
The two-handed scraper is a very useful tool—really good when you want to achieve a vigorous nonsanded character finish. Work with a light pushing cut, with the tool moving diagonally to the run of the grain. Aim for long, wide silky shavings.

Shaped
The best way we've found for scraping moldings is to grind the back edge of an old paint graining tool to fit the molded profile.

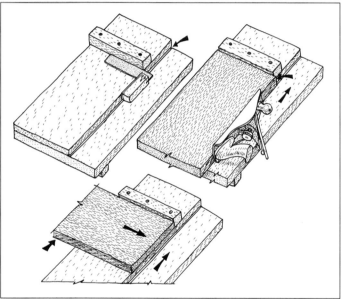

SHOOTING BOARD
This is a piece of equipment used for squaring the edge or end of a board.

Top left, a shooting board is pretty easy to make. Ours is a piece of plywood about 9 inches wide and 24 inches long, with a chamfer along the bottom edge. All the edges and faces are true and square.

Top right, to use, wax the lower run with a candle. Position and hold the workpiece so that the edge to be worked is hanging over the run, and use the plane on its side.

Bottom, to trim end grain, the board is held more or less flush with the stop, so as to avoid doing damage when the plane comes to the end of its run.

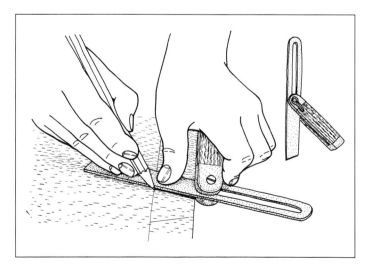

SLIDING BEVEL
The sliding bevel has a loose blade that slides and pivots. It's a good tool for marking out dovetails.

SPOKESHAVE

In many ways we often prefer to use an old wooden spokeshave for general shaping, especially for round nosings. We tend to use it instead of a drawknife.

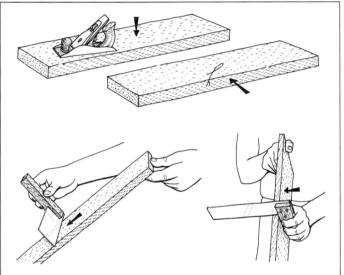

SQUARING

Squaring is the procedure for achieving a true face and edges.

Top, first plane the face to a true finish, then use it as a reference for planing the other faces and edges.

Bottom left, use a square to test for ripples and high spots.

Bottom right, to check for face-to-edge squareness, hold the square firmly against both surfaces and slightly rock the tool. If light shows between the tool and the face being worked, the wood is still uneven.

SURFACE PLANER

If you are a beginner and want to shortcut the planing procedure, get a small portable surface planer. Our planer, shown here, is a gem. The rough wood goes in one end and comes out looking silky smooth—beautiful!

TRANSFERRING DESIGNS

To transfer traced designs onto the surface of the wood, first make a tracing with a soft pencil, then reverse the tracing and align it with guidelines you've made on the workpiece. Secure it in place with pieces of masking tape, and go over the lines with a hard pencil. If you want to speed up the drawing and tracing procedure, you can use a photocopy machine to enlarge the design directly from the book.

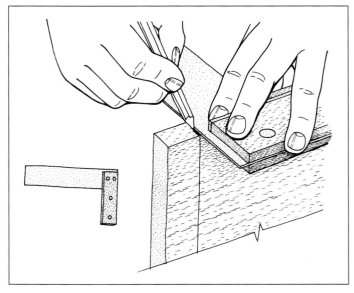

TRY SQUARE

This tool is used for testing for squareness, for drawing right angles, and for generally setting out joints.

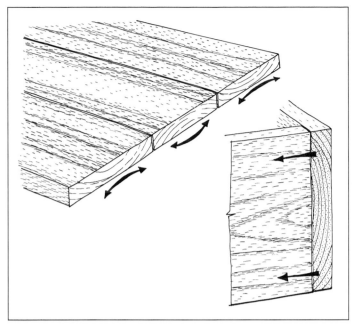

Warping Boards

Wood expands and contracts throughout its life, with the resultant warping greatly affecting the success of the finished boxes and chests.

Left, boards warp in the opposite direction to the curve of the annual rings, meaning back from the center of the tree. The best arrangement when edge-jointing a number of boards is to have a counterchange, so that the movement of neighboring boards counteract each other.

Right, as the cause of most joint failure has to do with the wood moving, the best prevention is to assemble the boards so that the grain direction is parallel on both pieces.

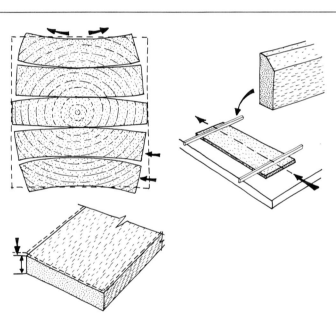

Winding, Twisting, and Shrinking

If your boards aren't quite right, chances are that they are winded or twisted.

Top left, seasoned boards tend to shrink as they dry out, with the effect that they curve away from the center and twist.

Right, use a couple of battens to test for winding. Set the sticks apart and at right angles to the edge of the board and parallel to each other. Sight down the length of the board and across the sticks. If you can't get the sticks to line up, the board is twisted and warped.

Bottom, a big mistake made by beginners is that they fail to take into account that wood sizes shrink when they have been planed, and boards that you buy are actually about 1/4 inch smaller in each dimension than they are labeled. For example, when you buy a prepared 1-by-6-inch plank—meaning a plank labeled and described as 1 inch thick and 6 inches wide—what you actually get is a plank that measures about 3/4 inch thick and 53/4 inches wide.

Reading List

Allen, Sam. *Plane Basics*. New York: Sterling, 1993.

Bridgewater, Alan, and Gill Bridgewater. *Folk Art Woodcarving: 832 Detailed Patterns*. New York: Sterling, 1990.

———. *Painted Wood Projects in the Pennsylvania Folk Art Style*. New York: Sterling, 1995.

———. *Woodcarving Basics*. New York: Sterling, 1996.

Hawes, Kettel Russel. *The Pine Furniture of Early New England*. New York: Dover, 1956.

Knell, David. *English Country Furniture: The National and Regional Vernacular 1500–1900*. London: Barrie & Jenkins, 1995.

Lipman, Jean, and Alice Winchester. *The Flowering of American Folk Art*. New York: Viking, 1974.

Shea, John G. *Antique Country American Furniture of North America*. New York: Van Nostrand Reinhold, 1975.

Swank, Scott T. *Arts of the Pennsylvania Germans*. New York: W. W. Norton & Co., 1983.

Metric Conversions

INCHES TO MILLIMETERS

IN.	MM	IN.	MM	IN.	MM	IN.	MM
1	25.4	26	660.4	51	1295.4	76	1930.4
2	50.8	27	685.8	52	1320.8	77	1955.8
3	76.2	28	711.2	53	1346.2	78	1981.2
4	101.6	29	736.6	54	1371.6	79	2006.6
5	127.0	30	762.0	55	1397.0	80	2032.0
6	152.4	31	787.4	56	1422.4	81	2057.4
7	177.8	32	812.8	57	1447.8	82	2082.8
8	203.2	33	838.2	58	1473.2	83	2108.2
9	228.6	34	863.6	59	1498.6	84	2133.6
10	254.0	35	889.0	60	1524.0	85	2159.0
11	279.4	36	914.4	61	1549.4	86	2184.4
12	304.8	37	939.8	62	1574.8	87	2209.8
13	330.2	38	965.2	63	1600.2	88	2235.2
14	355.6	39	990.6	64	1625.6	89	2260.6
15	381.0	40	1016.0	65	1651.0	90	2286.0
16	406.4	41	1041.4	66	1676.4	91	2311.4
17	431.8	42	1066.8	67	1701.8	92	2336.8
18	457.2	43	1092.2	68	1727.2	93	2362.2
19	482.6	44	1117.6	69	1752.6	94	2387.6
20	508.0	45	1143.0	70	1778.0	95	2413.0
21	533.4	46	1168.4	71	1803.4	96	2438.4
22	558.8	47	1193.8	72	1828.8	97	2463.8
23	584.2	48	1219.2	73	1854.2	98	2489.2
24	609.6	49	1244.6	74	1879.6	99	2514.6
25	635.0	50	1270.0	75	1905.0	100	2540.0

The above table is exact on the basis: 1 in. = 25.4 mm

U.S. TO METRIC
1 inch = 2.540 centimeters
1 foot = .305 meter
1 yard = .914 meter
1 mile = 1.609 kilometers

METRIC TO U.S.
1 millimeter = .039 inch
1 centimeter = .394 inch
1 meter = 3.281 feet or 1.094 yards
1 kilometer = .621 mile

INCH–METRIC EQUIVALENTS

FRACTION	DECIMAL EQUIVALENT		FRACTION	DECIMAL EQUIVALENT	
	CUSTOMARY (IN.)	METRIC (MM)		CUSTOMARY (IN.)	METRIC (MM)
1/64	.015	0.3969	33/64	.515	13.0969
1/32	.031	0.7938	17/32	.531	13.4938
3/64	.046	1.1906	35/64	.546	13.8906
1/16	.062	1.5875	9/16	.562	14.2875
5/64	.078	1.9844	37/64	.578	14.6844
3/32	.093	2.3813	19/32	.593	15.0813
7/64	.109	2.7781	39/64	.609	15.4781
1/8	.125	3.1750	5/8	.625	15.8750
9/64	.140	3.5719	41/64	.640	16.2719
5/32	.156	3.9688	21/32	.656	16.6688
11/64	.171	4.3656	43/64	.671	17.0656
3/16	.187	4.7625	11/16	.687	17.4625
13/64	.203	5.1594	45/64	.703	17.8594
7/32	.218	5.5563	23/32	.718	18.2563
15/64	.234	5.9531	47/64	.734	18.6531
1/4	.250	6.3500	3/4	.750	19.0500
17/64	.265	6.7469	49/64	.765	19.4469
9/32	.281	7.1438	25/32	.781	19.8438
19/64	.296	7.5406	51/64	.796	20.2406
5/16	.312	7.9375	13/16	.812	20.6375
21/64	.328	8.3384	53/64	.828	21.0344
11/32	.343	8.7313	27/32	.843	21.4313
23/64	.359	9.1281	55/64	.859	21.8281
3/8	.375	9.5250	7/8	.875	22.2250
25/64	.390	9.9219	57/64	.890	22.6219
13/32	.406	10.3188	29/32	.906	23.0188
27/64	.421	10.7156	59/64	.921	23.4156
7/16	.437	11.1125	15/16	.937	23.8125
29/64	.453	11.5094	61/64	.953	24.2094
15/32	.468	11.9063	31/32	.968	24.6063
31/64	.484	12.3031	63/64	.984	25.0031
1/2	.500	12.7000	1	1.000	25.4000